# Managing
# ADHD
## In School

### The Best Evidence-Based
### Methods for Teachers

# Russell Barkley, PhD

Internationally recognized authority on ADHD in children and adults

"Dr. Barkley has created a straightforward guide of best practices all educators should use with youth with ADHD. Included in the book are practical suggestions ranging from ways to better structure the classroom up to interventions that can be readily implemented in most classroom settings to promote academic productivity and appropriate behavior. This is a must read for educators, administrators, and parents/professionals working with youth with ADHD in schools!"

- **Gregory Fabiano, PhD,** Professor of Counseling, School, and
Educational Psychology, University at Buffalo, State University of New York

"*Managing ADHD in School* should be on the shelves of every educator who works with students with ADHD. It provides a concise, readable, and extremely practical guide to understanding and supporting the school success of students with ADHD. All of the recommendations provided in this timely resource are firmly grounded in empirical research; yet these are translated into practices that can be readily implemented in all school classrooms. It is particularly noteworthy that Managing ADHD in School provides a guide for effective assessment and intervention across elementary, middle, and high school settings. Dr. Barkley has produced the definitive guide to ADHD for general and special education teachers as well as school professionals (e.g., school psychologists, counselors) who consult with teachers."

- **George J. DuPaul, PhD,** Professor
School Psychology, Lehigh University

"*Managing ADHD in School* is an excellent resource for teachers on the *what* and *why* of effective school practices for ADHD. Dr. Barkley, a foremost expert in the field, provides highly readable, interesting, and authoritative information about the neurodevelopmental basis for ADHD and the executive functioning and self-regulation deficits plaguing students with ADHD. This book clearly describes which teaching methods are effective for managing these deficits and why they will work. A wealth of practical, research-supported teaching strategies that can be readily applied in classrooms fill the pages. In addition, teachers will benefit from the detailed information about the latest medications for ADHD. This book will be extremely useful for teachers—easy-to-read, practical, and provides teachers with exactly what they need to know to best help their students with ADHD!"

- **Linda J. Pfiffner, PhD,** Professor, Department of Psychiatry,
University of California, San Francisco

Copyright © 2016 by Russell Barkley, PhD

Published by
PESI Publishing & Media
PESI, Inc
3839 White Ave
Eau Claire, WI 54703

Cover: Amy Rubenzer
Editing: Bookmasters
Layout: Bookmasters & Amy Rubenzer

ISBN: 9781559570435

Printed in the United States of America.

PESI
Publishing
& Media
www.pesipublishing.com

# Table of Contents

# About the Author

 **Russell A. Barkley, PhD**, is a Clinical Professor of Psychiatry at the Medical University of South Carolina. He holds a Diplomate (board certification) in three specialties, Clinical Psychology, Clinical Child and Adolescent Psychology, and Clinical Neuropsychology. Dr. Barkley is a clinical scientist, educator, and practitioner whose publications include 22 other books, rating scales, and clinical manuals including the internationally acclaimed professional textbook, *Attention Deficit Hyperactivity Disorder: A Handbook for Diagnosis and Treatment*, now in its fourth edition (Guilford Press, 2015). He has also published more than 275 scientific articles and book chapters related to the nature, assessment, and treatment of ADHD and related disorders. He is the founder and editor of the clinical newsletter, *The ADHD Report*, now in its 24th year of publication.

Dr. Barkley has designed and managed classrooms in schools as part of his federally funded research on early school interventions for children with ADHD. He has also consulted with thousands of schools on the management of children with ADHD seen in his clinical practice. And he has trained thousands of school-based professionals about ADHD through his workshops. Dr. Barkley has presented more than 800 invited addresses internationally and appeared on nationally televised programs such as *60 Minutes, Today Show, Good Morning America, CBS Sunday Morning, CNN*, and many other television and radio programs in order to disseminate science-based information on ADHD. He has received numerous awards from professionals associations for his career accomplishments. His websites are www.russellbarkley.org and www.ADHDLectures.com.

# Acknowledgments

I wish to thank Linda Jackson with PESI for appreciating the need for a detailed explication of methods that teachers can use to manage ADHD in the school setting and her subsequent support and encouragement of this book. I am, as always, especially grateful to my wife, Pat, for not just her patience with and support of my writing this book, but for creating our home and especially for blessing that home with our two sons, Steve and Ken. Our son, Steve and wife Laura, have further bequeathed such blessings to us with their own sons, Liam and Craig. All bring much thoughtfulness, affection, care, laughter, learning, and love to my life. For all that and more I am eternally grateful.

*Russell A. Barkley, PhD*
*Charleston, SC*

# Foreword

Although I have written many books for clinical professionals, parents of children with ADHD, adults with ADHD, and loved ones of adults with ADHD, this is my first book designed specifically for educators. I wrote this book for teachers because I know firsthand that they serve on the front lines of dealing with the educational problems that the vast majority of children with ADHD are likely to experience across their schooling.

Another motivation for doing so was that **the educational domain is the most impaired by ADHD and is impaired in the highest percentage of children and teens with ADHD than is any other domain of major life activities. Over 90 percent of children and teens with ADHD will experience classroom behavioral and emotional problems, peer relationship problems in the school, low academic achievement, or various adverse consequences associated with these difficulties**, such as grade retention, placement in formal special educational services, and school suspensions and expulsions. Between 30 – 40 percent of them will not complete compulsory education in the United States because of these ADHD-related problems in school. Only 5–10 percent will complete a college education, which is 3–7 times less than the national average in the United States. In short, if ever there was a major domain of life that cries out for assistance for children and teens with ADHD, it is in school.

**Other books deal with ADHD in schools, so why read this one?**

What makes this book unique is that it goes beyond just describing the various and obvious problems children and teens with ADHD manifest in school. Other books explain what problems are associated with ADHD in the classroom, too. But **this one goes beyond the "what" in order to explain "why" those problems are likely to exist**. It tells you about the underlying neuropsychological difficulties in ADHD that create the various school-based problems seen in most children and teens with the disorder.

ADHD is far more than just a problem with attention, hyperactivity, or impulsiveness. It is a disorder of the brain's executive system – a system essential for effective functioning in school and in most other important domains of life (see Chapter 3 for more details on the brain's involvement in ADHD). As you will learn, ADHD disrupts the normal development of the brain's executive functions, meaning that ADHD is really an executive function deficit disorder (EFDD). And because the executive system is the basis for self-regulation, ADHD is also self-regulation deficit disorder (SRDD). This explains why ADHD is one of the most impairing if not THE most impairing psychological disorder we routinely treat on an outpatient basis in clinical psychology and psychiatry.

**Seeing the "why" behind the "what" can better help both educators and clinicians to understand the reasons behind not only the problematic behavior of a child or teen with ADHD in the classroom but also the "why" behind the choice of specific intervention methods.** It not only sets out what educators can do to help, but just as important, why those methods are likely to be effective. Moreover, by understanding the "why" – the reasons for the problems and for the treatments – educators can appreciate the principles underlying these treatments and so use those principles to develop new interventions on their own.

For instance, teachers are often told to increase the frequency of consequences, to shorten work quotas, to allow frequent exercise breaks, or to add more structure (whatever that is) to the child's work area for children and teens with ADHD, among other stock recommendations. Why? Why should we do this for them when we don't do it for other children? The standard answer is because it works. That may be true, but don't you think it is even better to know why something works than just that it might work? Doesn't knowing the reasons behind the effectiveness of a treatment give us more understanding and power to develop even more and better therapies?

Consider the classic case of how the British Navy learned that citrus fruits such as limes and lemons would treat scurvy. Yes, they learned eventually that it would work by simply giving them to some sailors and not others. But they didn't know why it worked. Once they learned about the role of vitamin deficiency in causing scurvy, they and all other sailors were better able to not just treat scurvy but to prevent it. And that led to treating and even preventing other vitamin deficiency syndromes. It is the same situation with ADHD.

Knowing the "why it happens" behind the "what happens" can greatly improve the effectiveness of current therapies and even lead to our developing new and better ones. Here I will tell you the "why" behind the problems shown by children and teens with ADHD in school, empowering you to be not only more knowledgeable about the nature of ADHD but to be far more effective in dealing with those problems.

What also makes this book unique is that I won't waste your time with a lot of narrative prose, needlessly detailed explanations, study-by-study research findings, and reference citations. You are far too busy for such excessiveness. Here I will get right to the point, setting out in the chapters what problems ADHD poses for children and teens in school, why those problems occur, what you should do about them, and why those things should be done. I will be nothing here if not direct with you. Within will be the critical pieces of information you need to have, along with bulleted lists of effective methods you can use, and crisp, clear statements of the steps you need to follow to implement those methods. Nothing more. If you want stories, you can always read a good novel. But **if you want to know precisely what to do to help a child or teen with ADHD in your classroom and why you need to do it, this book is definitely for you**.

This book provides an array or buffet of what can be done to address the problems and so achieve your goals of helping a child or teen with ADHD in your classroom. Of course, I don't expect you to undertake all of these methods. What steps to take depend, of course, on the child's specific school problem, his or her grade level and maturity, the time, opportunity, and resources you have to implement those steps, school policies, and, in some cases, the cooperation of parents to assist with any steps.

As you know already, in designing a program to help any child, context is everything. So I give you a wide array of things to consider doing to help a child or teen with ADHD from which you can tailor what you believe to be the best plan for that child and context. I know that you know what is best for the child or teen you have in mind. And should you discover new ways to effectively treat a specific problem related to ADHD in your classroom that I did not cover here, please pass it along so I can do the same for other teachers in the next edition (my email address is drbarkley6769@comcast.net). Thanks!

# CHAPTER 1

# What is ADHD?

ADHD is a neurodevelopmental condition that consists of developmental delays or deficiencies in at least two types of neuropsychological abilities. These two dimensions are *inattention* and *hyperactive-impulsive* symptoms. The disorder is classified as *neuro*developmental because the scientific evidence for the substantial role of neurological and genetic causes in ADHD is now overwhelming and irrefutable. ADHD is considered to be neuro*developmental* because it is primarily the result of a delay or lag in specific mental abilities. Those deficits are largely due to delays and/or dysfunction in the maturation of the brain areas that underlie those abilities. Such brain maldevelopment seems to arise largely from genetics but can also occur as a consequence of damage or other disruptive influences experienced by the child or teen at any time during development but most often during prenatal brain formation.

The symptoms of ADHD are dimensional in that they reflect the extreme end of a continuum of normal or typical human ability in these two areas. Children and teens with ADHD have a disorder that:

- Is beyond their own choice or making.

- Is intrinsic to their psychological and physical nature.

- Is not a categorical condition, like being pregnant.

- Differs from the behavior and abilities of other students in these dimensions as a matter of degree (quantitative) not of kind (qualitative).

- Will become evident sometime during childhood development (before 16 years in 98% of all cases).

- Is likely to be pervasive across many but not necessarily all situations.

- Is likely to be persistent across development for many but not necessarily all cases.

# The Symptoms of ADHD

The symptoms most often evident in children and teens with ADHD include:

**Inattention:**

- Fails to give close attention to details

- Makes careless mistakes

- Cannot sustain attention to tasks or activities

- Doesn't seem to listen well

- Doesn't follow through on instructions

- Fails to finish work

- Cannot organize activities well

- Avoids or seems reluctant to engage in things requiring sustained effort

- Loses things necessary to complete tasks or activities

- Is easily distracted

- Forgets things

**Hyperactivity-Impulsivity:**

- Fidgets with hands or feet or squirms in seat

- Leaves seat when expected to remain seated

- Runs about or climbs on things where inappropriate to do so

- Is unable to play quietly

- Often seems to be "on the go" or "driven by a motor"

- Talks too much

- Blurts out answers prematurely

- Cannot wait

- Interrupts or intrudes on others' activities

These symptoms must occur at least often and to a degree that is excessive for their age. The child or teen exhibits a majority (6 or more) of the symptoms on either list. Several symptoms must have developed in childhood (before 12 years of age). These symptoms must have persisted for at least the past 6 months, must occur in two or more settings (home, school, work, community), and must lead to impaired functioning in major life activities, such as social (family, peers, community), academic, or occupational activities. Only a small percentage of children will meet all of these conditions, making those who do worse than 92–95 percent of the child or adolescent population in these respects.

## The Deficient Mental Abilities Contributing to the Symptoms

I and many other clinical researchers conceptualize these symptoms as involving deficits in the following mental abilities, often referred to as executive functions (read more about these and their brain networks in Chapter 3, What Causes ADHD?):

### *Goal-directed persistence (inattention) and resistance to distraction:*

What separates the attention problems seen in ADHD from those evident in other disorders, such as depression, is that those with ADHD have problems with sustaining attention to and persisting toward the future.

They are less able to persist at getting things done over time, in time, and on time that involve delayed or future events. They pay attention to what is happening now just fine but not to what they need to be doing to be ready for what is coming next or what they have been assigned to do. Even if they try to persist toward tasks or goals, they are more likely than others to react to distractions, which are events that are not relevant to the goal or task.

Those distracting events are not just irrelevant things occurring around them, but also irrelevant ideas occurring in their mind. The problem here is not one of detecting those distractors better than others but in failing to inhibit reacting to those distractors as well as others.

### *Working memory:*

A large part of their inattentiveness comes from the inability to hold in mind what goal they have chosen or been assigned, what that involves, and monitoring when it has been accomplished. This reflects a deficiency in working memory, which is remembering what to do.

Memory for facts, knowledge, or information is not so much the problem as remembering what is to be done and persisting at it until it is so. Even if they try to hold such information in mind in order to guide their behavior toward a goal or task, such as instructions or assignments you gave them, any distractions will disrupt and degrade this special type of memory. The mental chalkboard of working memory is wiped clean by the distraction, and so the child is now off doing something other than what he or she is supposed to be doing.

And having reacted to a distraction, and so gone "off-task," the child is far less likely to reengage the original and now uncompleted goal or task. In sum, children or teens with ADHD are less likely than others to remember what they were supposed to be doing. Yes, ADHD children are forgetful. But as you can see here, it is a special type of forgetfulness – it is forgetting what they are supposed to be doing (forgetting the future).

### Inhibition:

Children and teens with ADHD are not just impulsive (poorly inhibited) in their actions, which leads them to move around, touch things, and otherwise behave too much (the hyperactivity). Their deficit in inhibition extends to their verbal behavior (talking excessively) and to their cognitive activities or thinking (impulsive decision making). It also interferes with their self-motivation, meaning that they are more likely than others to opt for immediate rewards or gratification.

Put another way, they steeply discount the value of a future or delayed event or consequence (reward or punishment) more than others, causing them to have a high time preference – they prefer to have small results now rather than larger results later.

Finally, their impulsiveness is evident in their emotions. They are more likely to display their emotional reactions and do it more quickly than do others of their age. And, if strong emotions have been provoked by some event, they will have a far more difficult time moderating or otherwise self-regulating that emotion. So children with ADHD are less patient, more easily frustrated, quicker to arouse, more excitable, and sillier, yet also more likely to react with anger, and so more likely to respond with aggression when provoked. They show emotions that are less mature, appropriate and consistent with or supportive of their future welfare than others.

### Planning and problem solving:

ADHD is associated with difficulties in generating multiple possible options for overcoming obstacles encountered when pursuing goals or contemplating multiple solutions posed by problems.

A related deficit is in the ability to construct and execute the steps of a plan necessary to attain a goal. This difficulty is often evident in school settings in problems with mental arithmetic, verbal narratives to questions posed in class or on exams, oral reports, written reports, and other tasks in which a complex, well-organized response is necessary.

**If you noticed a recurring theme here, it is that ADHD interferes with thoughts, actions, words, motivations, and emotions aimed at organizing behavior across time and preparing for the future instead of just reacting to the moment**. To act impulsively, fail to persist, and be distractible is to be nearsighted to the future – to be preoccupied by moments and so be blind to time. The aforementioned cognitive deficits will then disrupt the student's executive functioning (EF) in daily school activities. Deficient executive functioning in daily life will be evident in problems with:

- *Self-restraint* – deficient behavioral inhibition, limited self-control, poor delay of gratification, and difficulties subordinating one's immediate interests and desires to those of others.

- *Self-management to time* – poor time management and organization across time to achieve one's goals or accomplish assigned tasks.

- *Self-motivation* – an inability to activate and sustain motivation to relatively boring, tedious, effortful, or lengthy tasks in which there is no intrinsic interest or immediate payoff.

- *Self-organization and problem solving* – difficulty with organizing one's personal space, desk, locker, academic materials, etc., so as to accomplish work efficiently and effectively. Forgetfulness of what is to be done or what was assigned will be commonplace. As noted earlier, there will also be deficits evident in tasks that require working memory and thoughtful problem solving.

- *Self-regulation of emotions* – difficulty with inhibiting the expression of impulsive emotions in reaction to emotionally provocative events. This is evident in the student being easily excitable, prone to both positive and negative emotional outbursts, and greater-than-typical impatience, frustration, anger, hostility, and reactive aggression.

The vast majority of children and teens meeting research diagnostic criteria for ADHD fall in the bottom 7 percent of the population in each of these major areas of executive functioning in daily life. It is easy to see how such deficits would produce a myriad of difficulties with functioning in educational settings that typically place a premium on these EF abilities.

## CHAPTER 2

# The Facts About ADHD

- 5–8% of children and 4–7% of teens have ADHD (as do 3–5% of adults).

- The prevalence of ADHD therefore declines somewhat with age, which implies that some children with ADHD will recover from the disorder by adulthood (estimated to be 10–34% depending on one's definition of recovery).

- Hyperactive symptoms decline more steeply with age than do the inattention symptoms.

- But the number of domains of daily life impaired by ADHD can increase with age because more domains become available for participation than in childhood (e.g., sex, driving, work, managing money, cohabiting with a partner, raising children, etc.).

- In some regions, the prevalence of ADHD may be higher, such as in dense urban centers with higher rates of poverty, blue-collar or lower-middle social class neighborhoods, areas surrounding military bases, or regions that have more of the factors that can cause ADHD (toxins, poor prenatal care, more smoking or alcohol use during pregnancy, etc. – see Chapter 3). The reason ADHD may be more common among the children of certain occupational groups is because more adults with ADHD are likely to be in those occupations. Given the high genetic contribution to ADHD, those adults are more likely to have children with ADHD.

- The sex ratio of ADHD is 3–4:1 (males to females) in children, 2–2.5:1 in adolescence, and nearly 1.5:1 in adulthood. The reason for the convergence of the sex difference across development is unknown at this time.

- The nature of the symptoms of ADHD itself is not different between boys and girls. However, the other disorders or impairments that can coexist with ADHD, such as aggression or depression, maybe more or less common depending on the sex of the child.

    Boys with ADHD may be more likely to have aggressive or antisocial behavior, more likely to engage in risk taking, and be more at risk for later driving problems, drug use, and addiction than are girls with ADHD. Girls with ADHD may be more likely to experience peer problems or rejection, depression, anxiety disorders, binge eating pathology or bulimia, and possibly academic failure (though this is arguable) than boys with the disorder. Both sexes having ADHD are more prone to all of these coexisting problems than are typical boys or girls.

7

There is no evidence of significant or meaningful differences in prevalence or in the nature of the disorder across ethnic groups. In some places where an ethnic group may seem to have more ADHD than usual, it is typically because of the other factors already noted that may affect prevalence in a region. It is not due to some propensity for that ethnic or racial group to have more ADHD due merely to their ethnic or racial background.

In any given region, the number of children who are actually clinically referred and diagnosed with the disorder may be more or less than the prevalence within those regions. Rates of clinical diagnosis are not the same as rates of true disorder. Some regions have few medical or psychological professionals, have professionals that are less trained in ADHD, have parents and schools that are less knowledgeable or aware of ADHD, or may have few resources for clinical evaluations and treatment of it. There, rates of diagnosis of ADHD may be well below the actual prevalence level for the disorder in that region.

In regions with greater economic wealth, the opposite patterns to those above may occur. That is, rates of diagnosis may match or even exceed the rates of prevalence. In upper income neighborhoods where a premium is placed on academic excellence or acceleration, rates of diagnosis may even be higher than the rates of prevalence because parents (and schools) can pressure doctors to diagnose marginal (or even fictitious) cases of the disorder that don't meet all the criteria for having ADHD. This can happen when parents want performance-enhancing medications and/or educational accommodations for their child so she or he can outperform other children.

## Setting Factors That Influence ADHD Severity

Children and teens with ADHD may show significant fluctuations in the severity of their symptoms across diverse situations or settings. In general, symptoms of ADHD may often be worse in settings or tasks that:

- Are boring or uninteresting.
- Involve significantly delayed consequences or infrequent feedback.
- Require working independently of others.
- Lack supervision.
- Involve groups of children.
- Are highly familiar (and thus usually less interesting).
- Involve parents rather than strangers or less familiar adults.
- Include parents or supervisors who talk and reason too much but rarely act to control misbehavior.
- Require waiting.
- Occur late in the afternoon or evening (due to fatigue in self-control).
- Place substantial restrictions on movement (like classroom desk work!).

All of these settings demand executive functioning and self-regulation. The symptoms of ADHD can be less debilitating in the settings that involve factors that are the opposite of those in the preceding list. Specifically, these best-case situations may involve fun activities, highly stimulating or interesting tasks (e.g., videogames), lots of movement (e.g., gym, recess, sports), frequent rewards or feedback, highly supervised settings, working in small teams with peers rather than independently, working one-on-one with an adult, highly novel settings, where supervisors speak briefly but back up their rules with consequences, and where there is little or no pressure to wait for things.

# CHAPTER 3

# What Causes ADHD?

ADHD is known as a neurodevelopmental disorder. Its chief causes exist in the broad realms of genetics and neurology rather than in the domain of social causes.

## Genetics

ADHD is a highly inherited disorder. For instance, if a parent has the diagnosis, that individual's children are 6–8 times more likely to have the disorder (35–54%). If a child has ADHD, a biological brother or sister is 3–5 times more likely to have the condition (25–35%). Their biological mother is 3–4 times more likely to have ADHD, and their biological father is 5–6 times more likely to have it. If an identical twin has ADHD, the other twin will be ADHD in 75–90 percent of cases. These statistics clearly show the genetic (heritable) nature of ADHD.

The degree to which individual differences in genes among people contributes to individual differences in their ADHD symptoms is 65–80 percent. In other words, as much as 80 percent of the differences among people in their degree of ADHD symptoms is due to differences in their genetic makeup. This proportion is higher than the genetic contribution to temperament and personality traits, depression, anxiety, antisocial behavior, and even intelligence. It is only slightly less than the genetic contribution to variation among people in their height.

Research currently suggests that as many as 25–44 genes may be involved in causing ADHD. These genes are not different from those seen in typical people. So no disease gene or genes for ADHD is associated with the disorder as may be seen in Tay-Sachs or other severe neurological disorders. What is involved in ADHD are different *versions* of the genes seen in typical people. For instance, children with ADHD may have a longer version of a gene than that seen in a typical child – this is often known as tandem repeats. For instance, typical children may get four or five copies of the gene side-by-side while children with ADHD may have seven or more copies, thus creating a longer version of this gene. Such variations in gene length and repetition are called polymorphisms. The different version of the gene in cases of ADHD leads to different proteins and other chemicals and those lead to different structural changes in the brain. And those differences make the brain's functioning different – sometimes different enough to create ADHD.

Also, this explanation does not mean that all 25 or more risk genes need to be present to create the disorder; only a subset could well cause it. It *does* mean that cases of ADHD will vary in which genes will lead to a particular individual's case of the disorder. For instance, as a hypothetical example, it may be that just 5–8 genes from among this pool are needed to be present to cause a case of ADHD to emerge. But which subset of 5–8 that any case gets from

11

this risk pool of ADHD genes may be different from the 5–8 genes that caused another case of the disorder. This genetic randomness further means that similar-appearing symptomatic cases of the disorder could still have different underlying genetics. Those differences could lead to either subtle or even important variations in the nature of a given individual's disorder (some individuals are more impulsive, others more inattentive), in the risks for other disorders (such as depression, learning disorders, smoking, or other substance abuse), in the consequences from the disorder (driving impairments, criminal behavior), and even responsiveness to different ADHD medications or other treatments.

Understanding the genetics of ADHD also helps us to understand why ADHD may be more likely to be affiliated with some other psychiatric disorders that share the same or similar underlying genes. Some of the risk genes for ADHD, for instance, have been found in reading disorders, autistic spectrum disorders, and bipolar disorder, while other genes are shared with oppositional defiant disorder, conduct disorder, and even nicotine dependence and alcoholism.

Because ADHD is a disorder that falls along a continuum or dimension and because it is inherited, one can see signs of an ADHD phenotype within a family having the genetic form of the disorder. That is to say that parents and siblings of a child with ADHD may be more likely to manifest some milder forms of the symptoms or traits of the disorder even if they don't meet all of the requirements for receiving a diagnosis of it. [Note: the same is true in autistic spectrum disorders, which are also strongly genetically influenced.]

Although most cases of ADHD are genetic and involve inheritance of the genes contributing to ADHD from parent to child, new cases of ADHD can arise in a family due to genetic mutations in ADHD-risk genes that occur in the parents' eggs or sperm. These mutations get passed along to the children, creating a new line of ADHD risk in the family even though the parents do not have the disorder or any elevated risk for it.

## Neurology

Hundreds of research studies employing a variety of methods for measuring brain structure, functioning, development, and connectedness (networks) now support the conclusion that ADHD is largely a neurologically caused disorder. At least five or six brain regions are reliably linked to the disorder. They are the prefrontal cortex, the anterior cingulate cortex (at the midline of the frontal lobes), the frontal section of the corpus callosum, the striatum, and the cerebellum. Less certain is whether the thalamus is involved. Interestingly, evidence suggests that the right side of the brain in some or most of these regions may be somewhat more involved in creating ADHD than the left. But both sides of these regions appear to be involved in the disorder. In general, the brains of children and teens with ADHD are about 3–10 percent smaller globally in gray matter (the material on the outside layer of the brain). But these five specific brain regions appear to be even smaller – about 15–30 percent smaller than normal for age.

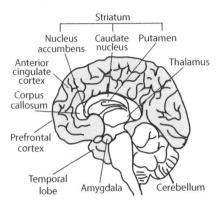

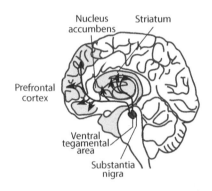

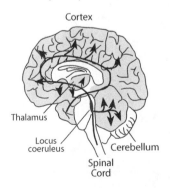

(A) Diagram of the human brain regions involved in ADHD.
(B) The dopamine system of the brain – a neurotransmitter system influenced by certain ADHD medications. (C) The norepinephrine system of the brain – a neurotransmitter system affected by other ADHD medications.
Source: http://ehp.niehs.nih.gov/

Developmental research finds the brain to be two–three years delayed in its development in these regions, especially the prefrontal lobes, and to be 10–30 percent less active than in typical comparison cases. More recently, fine-grained neuroimaging methods have revealed defective microstructures in the subcortical (white matter) neural networks that connect these brain regions to each other. These methods make the maturational deficiencies in ADHD even more obvious in the interconnectedness (networks) of these structures than was evident in studies of just surface gray matter. Although the size of the entire brain may eventually become closer to normal with age, the connectedness and functioning of the neural networks is likely to remain deficient for many cases into adulthood, though not for all cases. There is no doubt now that ADHD is of neurological origin, hence its classification as a *neurodevelopmental* disorder.

You can now understand why ADHD is both genetic and neurological. The genes involved in causing ADHD are genes that build and operate certain regions and networks in the brain during development. Versions of genes involved in ADHD that are different when compared to typical people result in differences and even deficiencies in these structures and their functioning. ADHD is therefore a neurogenetic disorder in many cases.

But ADHD can also arise from nongenetic sources. Most of these conditions or factors can potentially interfere with brain growth and functioning, especially in the ADHD-related brain regions. For example, it is now known that when a mother smokes tobacco or drinks alcohol beyond a certain amount during her pregnancy, she increases the risk for ADHD in her unborn child 2–3 times over the typical risk.

This increased risk is likely the result of the toxic effect these substances have on brain development. Other pregnancy complications may do much the same, abnormally altering brain development. These complications may include conditions such as the number of maternal infections during pregnancy, delivery complications, degree to which the baby was born substantially premature, degree of severe stress to which the mother was exposed during pregnancy, extent of abuse of other drugs besides tobacco and alcohol during pregnancy, and other factors. A smaller percentage of ADHD cases may be due to brain injuries suffered after the child is born, resulting from diseases, brain trauma, tumors, stroke, or even poisoning, such as with lead or pesticide exposure.

Most recently, some research shows that these environmental risk factors can interact with the ADHD risk genes discussed earlier to further heighten a child's risk for ADHD. This is illustrated in the chart below. For instance, if a mother passes one of the major ADHD risk-genes to her child *and* she smokes during that pregnancy, the risk for ADHD in her child is magnified by 2–3 times than would have been the case from either the risk-gene or maternal smoking alone (evidence of a risk-gene by environment interaction). In summary, about 60–70 percent of cases of ADHD are likely due to inheritance or genetic factors. Another 20–25 percent arise from pregnancy complications that may adversely affect brain development or that interact with ADHD risk genes to do so. The remaining 5–20 percent may arise from injuries to the brain sustained after birth.

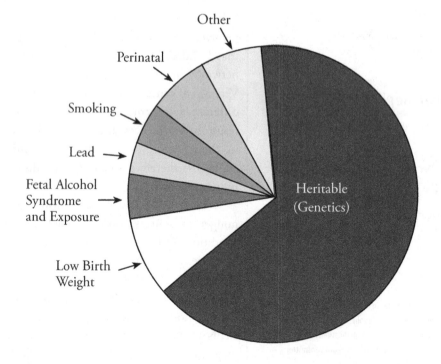

Causes contributing to ADHD. Joel Nigg (2006). What Causes ADHD? New York: Guilford Press. Copyright 2006 by Guilford Press. Reprinted with permission.

Notice here that no compelling evidence indicates that social factors, such as parenting or educational environment, have been found to cause ADHD. The degree of evidence against such explanations is now so compelling that no reputable scientist working in this field gives them any credence at this time. This does not mean that social factors are unimportant; just that they are not implicated in explaining the initial causes of ADHD. They are still important in determining how impaired someone with ADHD will be in specific situations. Social factors do exert an important influence in what a child's risk will be for other psychiatric disorders (e.g., anxiety, depression, oppositional behavior, conduct disorder, etc.). In addition, social environmental factors determine how much access to care children get for treating their ADHD and the quality of that care, including in the school setting.

# Prenatal & Early Devlopmental Risk

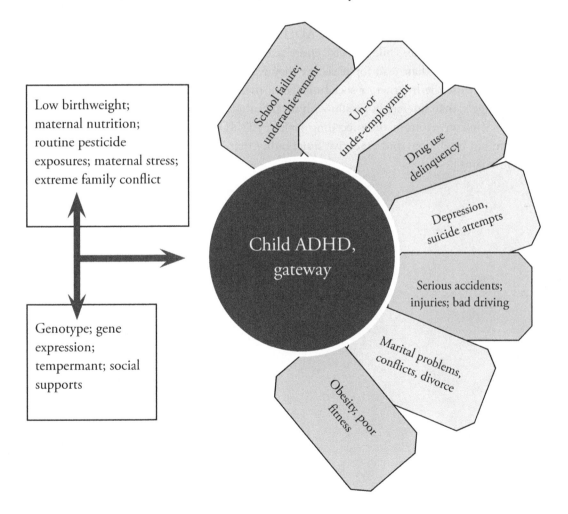

Low birthweight; maternal nutrition; routine pesticide exposures; maternal stress; extreme family conflict

Genotype; gene expression; tempermant; social supports

School failure; underachievement

Un-or under-employment

Drug use delinquency

Depression, suicide attempts

Serious accidents; injuries; bad driving

Child ADHD, gateway

Marital problems, conflicts, divorce

Obesity, poor fitness

Prenatal and early developmental risk  J. T. Nigg and R. A. Barkley (2013). Attention deficit–hyperactivity disorder. In E. J. Mash and R. A. Barkley (Eds.), Child Psychopathology, 3rd ed. New York: Guilford Press. Copyright 2013 by Guilford Press. Reprinted with permission.

Research has now ruled out the likelihood that dietary substances such as sugar or food preservatives and additives cause ADHD. Some children may be sensitive to food colorings enough to induce or mildly worsen their ADHD symptoms, but such effects are found in a minority of children and often when they are preschoolers, not when they are teens or adults. Antioxidants have not been found to be linked to ADHD and thus taking food supplements that increase them in the body seems unlikely at this time to benefit children with ADHD. Iron deficiencies have been found in some studies in children with ADHD, but this finding is not reliable across studies, and it is not clear that iron supplements would be helpful for management of the disorder in these cases.

ADHD does not arise from watching TV excessively, using computers too frequently, or playing videogames. Although degree of TV viewing in the early preschool years was correlated to a small degree with inattention in some studies; other studies completely failed to replicate that finding. And the direction of causation is also unclear here. We know that children with ADHD like to watch TV more than typical children, so ADHD could be leading to more TV viewing. The disorder is certainly associated with increased use of the Internet or videogames, but these don't cause ADHD – rather, ADHD predisposes children to excessive electronic media use. For instance, children with short attention spans would rather play a fast-paced exciting videogame than read for pleasure; they would rather watch TV than exercise; they would rather use the Internet or social media on their smartphones to socialize with others, even strangers, than interact in person with neighborhood or school-based peers.

As you can see from the preceding review, ADHD is a neurodevelopmental disorder of attention, inhibition, and executive functioning that largely arises from neurological and genetic origins.

# CHAPTER 4

# Principles for Managing the Executive Function Deficits in ADHD

Children and teens with ADHD have serious deficits in their executive functioning and self-regulation. In dealing with these deficits, several basic principles are important to keep in mind in constructing specific interventions for the educational problems of children and teens with ADHD.

Here are the principles that underlie the effective management of ADHD-related executive function (EF) deficits in the schools:

- Externalize Information

- Externally Represent or Remove Gaps in Time

- Externalize Motivation

- Executive Function and Self-Regulation: The Five Pathways to Change EF

- Make Problem-Solving Manual

- Intervene at the Point of Performance in Natural Settings

- Approach ADHD and Its EF Deficites as a Chronic Condition

## Externalize Information

> # Get Organized!
>
> → Plan Ahead
>
> → Make A To Do List
>
> → Write Down Assignments And Due Dates
>
> → Stay Ahead By Studying A Little Each Day
>
> → Make A Schedule And Stick To IT
>
> → Reward Yourself For Your Hard Work

If the process of regulating behavior by internally represented forms of information (i.e., working memory) is impaired or delayed in those with ADHD and its EF deficits, then those students will be best assisted by "externalizing" those forms of information. Providing physical representations of that information will be needed in the setting at the point of performance. Because covert or private information is weak as a source of stimulus control, making that information overt and public may assist with strengthening control of behavior. Make the information physical and place the physically represented information outside the child just as it has to have been in earlier development.

Everything that is internal in the content of our mind began as external information. The internal forms of information generated by the executive system, if they have been generated at all, appear to be extraordinarily weak in their ability to control and sustain the behavior toward the future in those with EF deficits. That behavior remains largely under the control of the salient aspects of the immediate context. So, make the information external again.

The solution to this problem of not being able to hold mental information in mind in ADHD is not to nag those with ADHD to simply try harder or to remember what they are supposed to be working on or toward. Instead, the solution is to fill the immediate context with physical cues comparable to the internal counterparts that are proving so ineffective. In a sense, clinicians treating those with EF deficits must beat the environment at its own game.

Whenever possible, minimize sources of high-appealing distracters that may subvert, distort, or disrupt task-directed mentally represented information and the behavior it is guiding. In their place should be cues, prompts, and other forms of information that are just as salient and appealing yet are directly associated with or are an inherent part of the task to be accomplished. Such externalized information serves to cue the individual to do what they know.

If the rules that are understood to be operative during educational activities, for instance, do not seem to be controlling the child's behavior, the rules should be "externalized." They can be externalized by posting signs about the school environment and its rules and have the student frequently refer to them. Having the student verbally self-state these rules aloud before and during individual work performances may also be helpful. One can also record these reminders on a digital recorder that the student listens to through an earphone while working.

## Externally Represent or Remove Gaps in Time

The organization of the individual's behavior both within and across time is one of the ultimate disabilities rendered by ADHD. EF deficits create problems with time, timing, and timeliness of behavior such that they are to time what nearsightedness is to spatial vision. They create a temporal myopia in which the individual's behavior is governed even more than normal by events close to or within the temporal now and the immediate context rather than by internal information that pertains to longer term, future events.

This helps to understand why students with EF deficits make the decisions they do, shortsighted as they seem to be to others around them. If one has little regard for future events, then much of one's behavior will be aimed at maximizing the immediate rewards and escaping from immediate hardships or aversive circumstances without concern for the delayed consequences of those actions.

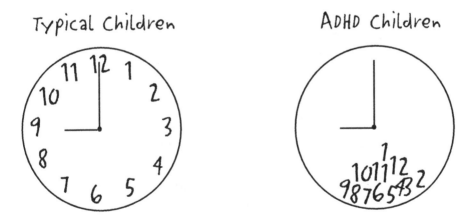

Those with deficient EF could be assisted by making time itself more externally represented, by reducing or eliminating gaps in time among the components of a behavioral contingency (event-response-outcome). Caregivers and others can also help to bridge such temporal gaps related to future events.

Another solution is to reduce or eliminate these problematic time-related elements of a task when feasible. The elements should be made more contiguous. Rather than tell the child that a project must be done over the next few days, week, or month, assist her with doing a step a day toward that eventual goal so that when the deadline arrives, the work has been done but done in small daily work periods with immediate feedback and incentives for doing so.

## Externalize Motivation

The EF theory of ADHD also hypothesizes that a deficit will exist in internally generated and represented forms of motivation needed to drive goal-directed behavior. Complaining to these children about their lack of motivation (laziness), drive, willpower, or self-discipline will not suffice to correct the problem. Pulling back from assisting them to let the natural consequences occur, as if this will teach them a lesson that will correct their behavior, is likewise a recipe for disaster. Instead, artificial means of creating external sources of motivation must be arranged at the point of performance in the context in which the work or behavior is desired.

For instance, providing artificial rewards, such as tokens, may be needed throughout the performance of a task or other goal-directed behavior when there is little or no immediate consequences associated with that performance. Such artificial reward programs become for the person with ADHD-related EF deficits what prosthetic devices are to the physically disabled, allowing them to perform more effectively in some tasks and settings with which they otherwise would have considerable difficulty. The motivational disability created by EF deficits makes such motivational prostheses essential for most children deficient in EF.

The methods of behavior modification are particularly well suited to achieving these ends. Many techniques for this form of treatment can be applied to children with ADHD-related EF deficits. First, it is important to recognize that (1) internalized, self-generated forms of motivation are weak at initiating and sustaining goal-directed behavior; (2) externalized sources of motivation, often artificial, must be arranged within the context at the point of performance; and (3) these compensatory, prosthetic forms of motivation must be sustained for long periods. If the external motivation is removed, the behavior will not be further sustained and the individual will regress to more erratic goal-directed behavior with less ability to sustain actions toward tasks and goals.

In general, there are two reasons to do behavior management for anyone: for informational training and for motivational sustaining. The former is done for individuals who have not yet acquired a skill. Once the skill is taught through behavioral or other pedagogical methods, those methods can be withdrawn and the behavior sustained presumably by contact with the natural contingencies. But in EF disorders like ADHD, the issue is not ignorance or lack of knowledge of a skill; the problems are with the skill's timing and execution at key points of performance and with the self-motivation needed to sustain the performance. Behavioral treatments can provide the motivational or behavior-sustaining assistance. Removing the external motivation after improvement in task performance will result in a loss of motivation and a return to the baseline state of limited self-motivation and an inability to sustain actions toward goals.

## Executive Function and Self-Regulation: The Five Pathways to Change EF

By equating EF with self-regulation (SR), and by viewing the SR of emotion as described by Gross as a specific form of a more generalized process of SR, the EF theory of ADHD illustrates at least five vectors through which EF/SR can influence goal-directed activities: situation selection, situation modification, attentional control/redirection, reappraisal, and response modification/suppression. In attempting to assist students with rehabilitating or at least compensating for their EF deficits, these five vectors offer opportunities in which clinicians can strive to overcome such deficits. Although this goal can be approached by directly working with the student, it is likely to be greatly assisted by advising caregivers to assist the individual with these five pathways of SR. Modifying the "point of performance" as discussed later on readily fits into the situation modification vector of SR. Various cognitive behavioral therapies may prove useful at the reappraisal pathway. The point here is not to map out all possible ways by which these five vectors of SR could be used to boost EF in those with EF deficits, but to make educators cognizant that such pathways are available.

Related to this idea of motivational deficits accompanying EF disorders such as ADHD is the self-regulatory strength and the resource pool of effort (willpower) associated with activities of SR. There is an abundant literature on this topic that has been overlooked by neuropsychologists studying EF, yet it has a direct bearing on EF given that EF is viewed as SR. Research indicates that each implementation of EF (working memory, inhibition, planning, reasoning, problem solving, etc.) depletes this limited resource pool temporarily such that protracted use of EF may greatly deplete the available pool of effort. This can result in students being less capable of SR (EF) in subsequent situations or immediately succeeding time periods. They are thus more likely to experience problems or fail outright in their efforts at EF/SR and resistance to immediate gratification. Such temporary depletions may be further exacerbated by stress, by alcohol or other drug use, by illness, and even from low levels of blood glucose.

Research also indicates what factors may serve to more rapidly replenish the resource pool. These include:

- Routine physical exercise.
- Taking 10 minute breaks periodically during SR strenuous situations.
- Relaxing or meditating for at least 3 minutes after such SR exerting activities.
- Visualizing the rewards or outcomes while involved in EF/SR tasks.

- Arranging for periodic small rewards throughout the tasks for SR-demanding settings.
- Engaging in self-affirming statements of self-efficacy prior to and during such tasks.
- Generating positive emotions.
- Consuming glucose-rich beverages during the task.

Some research further suggests that the actual capacity of the resource pool may be boosted by routine physical exercise and by routine practicing of tasks involving self-regulation daily for two weeks.

## Make Problem-Solving Manual

Children with ADHD cannot hold information in mind or manipulate mental information as well as other children. That means that mental problem solving is difficult for them. To assist them, try to think of ways to make the problem or the parts of the problem physical in various ways so that the child can manipulate those parts manually to facilitate mentally held information.

For instance, if they have mental arithmetic to do, let them have some marbles, a number line, an abacus, or some other way to physically count and manipulate the information to help them solve the math problems.

If the child has a written essay to do, encourage them to use 3 x 5 file cards and to write a different idea on each card as the ideas come to mind. Just have them think and free associate to the topic assigned to them. And as each idea is stated, have them write it down on a separate card. Now the child can take these "idea cards" and reorganize them into a possible essay on that topic.

I am sure you can think of other ways to do this for a child or teen with ADHD. Remember, it's not the method, but the principle to emphasize here: **make solving problems manual work and not just mental work**.

## Intervene at the Point of Performance in Natural Settings

Given the preceding principles, educators should likely reject most approaches to intervention for students with ADHD-related EF deficits that do not involve helping them with an active intervention at the point of performance. As noted, the point of performance is the place in the natural setting where the problem exists. It is there that intervention must occur if it is to address the problem in that situation.

Once-per-week tutoring is unlikely to succeed with the student with deficient EF without efforts to insert accommodations at key points of performance in natural settings to address the impaired domains of educational activities. This is not to say that extensive training or retraining of EF, as with working memory training, may not have some short-term benefits. Such practice has been shown to increase the likelihood of using working memory and of boosting the SR resource pool capacity in normal individuals, at least temporarily.

## Approach ADHD and Its
## EF Deficits as a Chronic Condition

The previous review of the etiologies of ADHD leads to a much more general implication – the approach taken to its management must be the same as that taken in the management of other chronic medical or psychiatric disabilities. Diabetes is an analogous condition to many forms of EF deficits. At the time of diagnosis, all involved must realize that there is currently no cure for the condition. Still, multiple means of treatment can provide symptomatic relief from the deleterious effects of the condition, including taking daily doses of medication and changing settings, tasks, and lifestyles.

Immediately following diagnosis, the clinician works to educate the patient and family on the nature of the chronic disorder, and then designs and implements a treatment package for the condition. This package must be maintained over long periods to sustain the symptomatic relief that the treatments initially achieve. Ideally, the treatment package, so maintained, will reduce or eliminate the secondary consequences of leaving the condition unmanaged.

However, each patient is different and so is each instance of the chronic condition being treated. As a result, symptom breakthroughs and crises are likely to occur periodically over the course of treatment that may demand reintervention or the design and implementation of modified or entirely new treatment packages. Changes to the environment that may assist those with the disorder are not viewed as somehow correcting earlier faulty learning or leading to permanent improvements that can permit the treatments to be withdrawn.

Instead, the more appropriate view of psychological treatment is one of designing a prosthetic educational environment that allows the student to better cope with and compensate for the disorder. Behavioral and other technologies used to assist people with ADHD-related EF deficits are akin to artificial limbs, hearing aids, wheel chairs, ramps, and other prostheses that reduce the handicapping impact of a disability and allow the individual greater access to and better performance of their major life activities. Those methods provide the additional social and cultural scaffolding around the student with EF deficits so that performance in that specific setting can be more effective.

# CHAPTER 5

# 10 Specific Rules for Managing ADHD

Based on the principles reviewed in the previous chapter for addressing EF deficits in children and teens with ADHD, one can develop 10 specific rules that need to be followed in setting up any program to address those deficits. They are:

1. ***Rules and instructions provided to children with ADHD must be clear, brief, and often delivered through more visible and external modes of presentation than is required for the management of children without ADHD.***

Stating directions clearly, having the child repeat them out loud, having the child utter them softly to themselves while following through on the instruction, and displaying sets of rules or rule-prompts (e.g., stop signs, big eyes, big ears for "stop, look, and listen" reminders) prominently throughout the classroom are essential to proper management of ADHD children. Relying on the child's recollection of the rules as well as upon purely verbal reminders is often ineffective.

> ## Classroom Rules
>
> 1. Listening Bodies
>    (I will Listen and follow Directions.)
>
> 2. Raised Hands
>    (I will raise my hand to share ideas)
>
> 3. Quiet Mouths
>    (I will use a soft voice.)

2. ***Represent time and time periods externally (physically).***

Children with ADHD are less capable of using their sense of time to manage their current behavior and get work done in time, over time, and on time. When short time intervals of an hour or less are required to do work, then represent that time period using a clock, kitchen timer, counting device or other external means to show the child how much time they have and how quickly it is passing. The large (1 ft.) clock at the addwarehouse.com can serve this purpose. Or just use a spring-loaded kitchen cooking-timer placed on the child's desk. For longer time periods, break the work down into shorter periods with smaller work quotas and allow the child to take frequent breaks between these shorter work periods.

3. *Consequences used to manage the behavior of ADHD children must be delivered swiftly and more immediately than is needed for children without ADHD.*

Delays in consequences greatly degrade their efficacy for children with ADHD. As will be noted throughout this chapter, the timing and strategic application of consequences with children with ADHD must be more systematic and are far more crucial to their management than in children without ADHD. This is not just true for rewards, but is especially so for punishment, which can be kept mild and still effective by delivering it as quickly upon the misbehavior as possible. Swift, not harsh, justice is the essence of effective punishment.

4. *Consequences must be delivered more frequently, not just more immediately, to children with ADHD in view of their motivational deficits.*

Behavioral tracking, or the ongoing adherence to rules after the rule has been stated and compliance initiated, appears to be problematic for children with ADHD. Frequent feedback or consequences for rule adherence seem helpful in maintaining appropriate degrees of tracking to rules over time.

5. *The type of consequences used with children with ADHD must often be of a higher magnitude, or more powerful, than that needed to manage the behavior of children without ADHD.*

The relative insensitivity of children with ADHD to response consequences dictates that those chosen for inclusion in a behavior management program must have sufficient reinforcement value or magnitude to motivate children with ADHD to perform the desired behaviors. Suffice it to say, then, that mere occasional praise or reprimands are simply not enough to effectively manage children with ADHD.

6. *An appropriate and often richer degree of incentives must be provided within a setting or task to reinforce appropriate behavior before punishment can be implemented.*

This means that punishment must remain within a relative balance with rewards or it is unlikely to succeed. It is therefore imperative that powerful reinforcement programs be established first and instituted over 1–2 weeks before implementing punishment in order for the punishment, sparingly used, to be maximally effective.

Often children with ADHD will not improve with the use of response cost or time-out if the availability of reinforcement is low in the classroom and hence removal from it is unlikely to be punitive. "Positives before negatives" is the order of the day with children with ADHD. When punishment fails, this is the first area that clinicians, consultations, or educators should explore for problems before instituting higher magnitude or more frequent punishment programs.

**7.** *Those reinforcers or particular rewards that are employed must be changed or rotated more frequently with children with ADHD than children without ADHD given the penchant of the former for more rapid habituation or satiation to response consequences, apparently to rewards in particular.*

This means that even though a particular reinforcer seems to be effective for the moment in motivating child compliance, it is likely that it will lose its reinforcement value more rapidly than normal. Reward menus in classes, such as those used to back up token systems, must therefore be changed periodically, say every 2–3 weeks, to maintain the power or efficacy of the program in motivating appropriate child behavior. Failure to do so is likely to result in the loss of power of the reward program and the premature abandonment of token technologies based on the false assumption that they simply will not work any longer.

Token systems can be maintained over an entire school year with minimal loss of power in the program provided that the reinforcers are changed frequently to accommodate to this problem of habituation. Such rewards can be returned later to the program once they have been set aside for a while, often with the result that their reinforcement value appears to have been improved by their absence or unavailability.

**8.** *Anticipation is the key with children with ADHD.*

This means that teachers must be more mindful of planning ahead in managing children with this disorder, particularly during phases of transition across activities or classes, to ensure that the children are cognizant of the shift in rules (and consequences) that is about to occur. It is useful for teachers to take a moment to prompt a child to recall the rules of conduct in the upcoming situation, repeat them orally, and recall what the rewards and punishments will be in the impending situation before entering that activity or situation.

Think aloud, think ahead is the important message to educators here. By themselves, such cognitive self-instructions are unlikely to be of lasting benefit, but when combined with contingency management procedures they can be of considerable aid to the classroom management of ADHD children. You will read more about this method in the Transition Planning chapter.

9. ***Children with ADHD must be held more publicly accountable more often for their behavior and goal attainment than children without ADHD.***

The weaknesses in executive functioning associated with ADHD result in a child whose behavior is less regulated by internal information (mental representations) and less monitored via self-awareness than is the case with children without ADHD.

Addressing such weaknesses requires that the child with ADHD be provided with more external cues about performance demands at key "points of performance" in the school, be monitored more closely by teachers, and be provided with consequences more often across the school day for behavioral control and goal attainment.

10. ***Behavioral interventions, while successful, only work while they are being implemented and, even then, require continued monitoring and modification over time for maximal effectiveness.***

One common scenario is that a student responds initially to a well-tailored program, but then over time, the response deteriorates; in other cases, a behavioral program may fail to modify the behavior at all. These outcomes do not mean behavioral programs do not work. Instead, such difficulties signal that the program needs to be modified. It is likely that one of a number of common problems (e.g., rewards lose their value, programs are not implemented consistently, or the program is not based on a functional analysis of the factors related to the problem behavior) occurred.

# CHAPTER 6

# Taking a Baseline Assessment of Problem Behavior

It can be especially helpful before you begin any interventions into the behavioral and academic problems of children with ADHD to evaluate the situations in school that are proving most problematic for them. First, this can serve as a baseline level of their problems against which you can then later evaluate the success of your interventions. A handy tool for this sort of quick assessment is the School Situations Questionnaire (see page 31) that I invented more than 30 years ago for just this purpose.

This rating scale lists 12 different situations in school settings in which children with ADHD may be having problems. It asks you to first indicate whether the situation is a problem for this child. Then you are to rate the degree of problematic behavior that occurs in each situation using a scale of 1 to 9.

## How To Score

If you wish, you can even score the scale to get two numbers. One is the number of problem settings ("yes" answers) and the second is the mean severity score. It is computed by adding up all of the ratings (circled numbers) across all of the situations which you indicated were a problem (Yes answers) for this child. Don't include the situations for which you answered "no", because those would not have been rated on the 1–9 scale. Then divide this sum by the number of problem settings (# of Yes answers). Save this scale as your baseline measure.

If you want to know just how unusual these scores are for this child compared to typical children, here is a rough guideline of cutoff scores for the scale. The numbers in the table are broken down separately for boys and girls and for two different age groups. If the child you have rated has a rating at or above these numbers for their age and sex, then that child is at or above the 93rd percentile for the population. That is a typical cutoff for determining if a child is having significant or "clinical levels" of problem behavior.

## Score Guidelines

| Age Range | Boys | | Girls | |
|---|---|---|---|---|
| | # of Problem Settings | Mean Severity | # of Problem Settings | Mean Severity |
| 6–8 | 7.4 | 4.5 | 4.0 | 3.1 |
| 9–11 | 7.6 | 5.1 | 4.5 | 2.6 |

After a few weeks of using the methods in this book to reduce a child's problematic behavior, complete a new assessment of the scale items. You can then compare it to your first ratings (baseline assessment) to see whether any improvement in the child's adjustment has taken place (a reduction in the ratings for each situation and in the two general scores).

# Sample
# School Situations Questionnaire

Child's name __Joe Smith__ Date __Jan. 1st__

Name of person completing this form __Jane Smith__

**Instructions:** Does this child present any problems with compliance to instructions, commands, or rules for you in any of these situations? If so, please circle the word Yes and then circle a number beside that situation that describes how severe the problem is for you. If this child is not a problem in a situation, circle No and go on to the next situation on the form.

| Situations | Yes/No | Mild | | | | If yes, how severe? | | | | Severe |
|---|---|---|---|---|---|---|---|---|---|---|
| When arriving at school | Yes (No) | 1 | 2 | 3 | 4 | 5 | 6 | 7 | 8 | 9 |
| During individual desk work | (Yes) No | 1 | 2 | 3 | 4 | 5 | (6) | 7 | 8 | 9 |
| During small group activities | Yes (No) | 1 | 2 | 3 | 4 | 5 | 6 | 7 | 8 | 9 |
| During free playtime in class | (Yes) No | 1 | 2 | 3 | 4 | 5 | 6 | 7 | (8) | 9 |
| During lectures to the class | (Yes) No | (1) | 2 | 3 | 4 | 5 | 6 | 7 | 8 | 9 |
| At recess | Yes (No) | 1 | 2 | 3 | 4 | 5 | 6 | 7 | 8 | 9 |
| At lunch | Yes (No) | 1 | 2 | 3 | 4 | 5 | 6 | 7 | 8 | 9 |
| In the hallways | Yes (No) | 1 | 2 | 3 | 4 | 5 | 6 | 7 | 8 | 9 |
| In the bathroom | (Yes) No | 1 | (2) | 3 | 4 | 5 | 6 | 7 | 8 | 9 |
| On field trips | Yes (No) | 1 | 2 | 3 | 4 | 5 | 6 | 7 | 8 | 9 |
| During special assemblies | Yes (No) | 1 | 2 | 3 | 4 | 5 | 6 | 7 | 8 | 9 |
| On the bus | Yes (No) | 1 | 2 | 3 | 4 | 5 | 6 | 7 | 8 | 9 |

- - - - - - - - - - - - - - - - - - - - - - - - - For Office Use Only - - - - - - - - - - - - - - - - - - - - - - - -

Total number of problem settings __4__

Mean severity score __4.25__

## School Situations Questionnaire

**Child's name**______________________________________________**Date**______________

Name of person completing this form__________________________________________

______________________________________________________________________________

**Instructions:** Does this child present any problems with compliance to instructions, commands, or rules for you in any of these situations? If so, please circle the word Yes and then circle a number beside that situation that describes how severe the problem is for you. If this child is not a problem in a situation, circle No and go on to the next situation on the form.

| | | | If yes, how severe? | | | | | | | | |
|---|---|---|---|---|---|---|---|---|---|---|---|
| **Situations** | **Yes/No** | | **Mild** | | | | | | | | **Severe** |
| When arriving at school | Yes | No | 1 | 2 | 3 | 4 | 5 | 6 | 7 | 8 | 9 |
| During individual desk work | Yes | No | 1 | 2 | 3 | 4 | 5 | 6 | 7 | 8 | 9 |
| During small group activities | Yes | No | 1 | 2 | 3 | 4 | 5 | 6 | 7 | 8 | 9 |
| During free playtime in class | Yes | No | 1 | 2 | 3 | 4 | 5 | 6 | 7 | 8 | 9 |
| During lectures to the class | Yes | No | 1 | 2 | 3 | 4 | 5 | 6 | 7 | 8 | 9 |
| At recess | Yes | No | 1 | 2 | 3 | 4 | 5 | 6 | 7 | 8 | 9 |
| At lunch | Yes | No | 1 | 2 | 3 | 4 | 5 | 6 | 7 | 8 | 9 |
| In the hallways | Yes | No | 1 | 2 | 3 | 4 | 5 | 6 | 7 | 8 | 9 |
| In the bathroom | Yes | No | 1 | 2 | 3 | 4 | 5 | 6 | 7 | 8 | 9 |
| On field trips | Yes | No | 1 | 2 | 3 | 4 | 5 | 6 | 7 | 8 | 9 |
| During special assemblies | Yes | No | 1 | 2 | 3 | 4 | 5 | 6 | 7 | 8 | 9 |
| On the bus | Yes | No | 1 | 2 | 3 | 4 | 5 | 6 | 7 | 8 | 9 |

-------------------------- For Office Use Only --------------------------

Total number of problem settings__________________

Mean severity score__________________

# CHAPTER 7

# Classroom Management Considerations

Consider the recommendations throughout the remainder of this book as you would a food buffet – choose from among these various methods those most suitable for the child or teen with ADHD you have in mind to help. I begin with some basic features of the classroom and teaching style that can help improve the school functioning of children and teens with ADHD.

In reviewing these, keep in mind an important distinction between proactive and reactive teaching methods. Many of the suggestions are examples of proactive teaching and behavior management. They are in contrast to the customary reactive approach many teachers take with ADHD students. Here, a change is made to a classroom situation or the curriculum or a plan is set up before any problem occurs. This approach reduces the likelihood of such problems happening in the upcoming situation.

Proactive teaching also increases the probability that appropriate behavior and school performance are likely to occur instead. I think you will agree that proactive methods are superior to reactive methods in dealing with students with ADHD as the former actually reduces or even prevents the likelihood that a problem will arise in a situation. The latter, reactive methods, only deal with it after it has occurred.

🖉 Have a school psychologist or master teacher knowledgeable in ADHD and school management methods serve as **a liaison or consultant to other teachers in the school who have ADHD children in their classrooms**. This consultant can provide basic information about ADHD to the teacher (such as found in Chapters 1–3) as well as make recommendations for specific classroom accommodations and behavior management strategies, such as those described in the remainder of this book.

🖉 **Don't retain a child in a grade!** Research shows it is associated with multiple harms and few if any benefits. Develop a real treatment plan instead repeating a failure.

🖊 Use the first few weeks of the school year to **establish behavioral control of the classroom**. Focus more on establishing clear rules and providing swift and reliable consequences for them. Give less emphasis to the curriculum or lesson plan and place more effort into establishing behavior management. Then you can gradually shift the emphasis to the content of the lesson plan.

🖊 **Decrease the child or teen's total workload** to what is essential rather than merely "busy" work assigned to fill class time. Ask yourself, "How much work does this student need to do to demonstrate that he or she has acquired the concept I am teaching?" That should be enough.

🖊 **Give smaller quotas of work at a time with frequent breaks** (i.e., 5 problems at a time, not 30, with short breaks between work episodes). For instance, take the worksheet of 30 math problems you want done and cut off the top row of 5 problems. Hand this snippet of work to the child to be done within the next few minutes. When they complete the work and bring it to you, then cut off the next row of 5 problems and assigned that work to them to be done within a few minutes. Continue this process until all of the problems are done.

  The principle to follow here is to assign smaller quotas of work at any one time, give a break, then assign another small quota. This makes the work fit within the child's attention span and so is more likely to get done.

🖊 Use a **traditional desk arrangement** in the classroom (all desks face forward to the teaching area).

🖊 **Seat the child with ADHD close to teaching area** to permit more supervision of and interaction with the child. It also provides you the capacity to engage in more frequent accountability of the child to you for his conduct and performance.

🖊 **Target productivity** (# of problems attempted) first and accuracy second. Start first by rewarding the child for each problem attempted and ignore the accuracy for the time being. Once productivity has improved, you can then increase your focus on the accuracy of the work being done. But if you focus on accuracy first (right or wrong), you will not encourage and may even punish productivity if you mark a few problems wrong.

🖊 **Don't send unfinished class work home for parents to do**. Parents of ADHD children have enough stress at home with the ordinary home responsibilities and school homework to be done and do not need to be overburdened with a teacher's failed responsibility.

- **Unfinished classwork shows that the problem lies at school in the classroom.** And that is where solutions are to be implemented and not shirked.

- **Give out weekly homework assignments** so parents can plan their week accordingly.

- **Reduce/eliminate homework for elementary kids** (research indicates that it benefits kids little before high school). If homework is to be given, keep it to 10 minutes total times the child's grade level in school (e.g., 10 minutes × third grade = 30 minutes total).

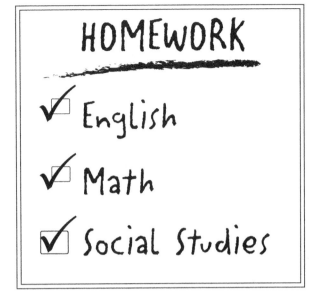

- **Allow some restlessness at the child's work area** or desk as long as she is working. Try letting the child squeeze a stress ball (rubber ball) in her non-dominant hand while she is working or let the child sit on a balance or exercise ball instead of a chair. This ball allows some movement to maintain stability while seated and can help the child concentrate on her work.

- **Give frequent but brief physical exercise breaks** throughout the school day.

✏ Get **color-coded binders** and other commercial organizing systems to help keep student materials and assignments better organized.

✏ Try letting students do **color-coding of text** that is to be read using highlighters for marking key points in the text. Then have the child write these highlighted key points down on paper after the reading is done.

✏ Use **participatory teaching**- give the student something useful and physically active to do to help you while teaching. This can be having the student stand next to you and hold the pointer while they point to material on the blackboard/whiteboard that you are currently discussing with the class. Or it can be having the student write key words or math problems down on the smartboard as you discuss that material.

✏ Let **students practice skills drills on computers** – let students use learning software programs to rehearse skills that have just been covered in class. Research shows that children with ADHD pay more attention to computer software learning programs and learn more from the practice with them than they do when working on mimeographed worksheets.

✏ **Discourage impulsive answers to questions**. Try using laminated work slates (whiteboards) about 1 ft. × 1 ft. in size. Each child gets a small whiteboard and marker and when questions are asked, everyone writes the answer on his or her board and holds it up in the air. Then you can call on someone only after ALL boards are up. That student can then explain to the class how he or she got that correct answer.

✏ **Assign a homework "study-buddy."**
This is like peer tutoring (discussed later) but done outside of school. Have children living near each other from the same class do their homework together, alternating whose home they meet at to do so.

- **Alternate low-appeal with high-appeal activities** within your classroom to maintain the children's interest level. Too many boring topics or activities back to back can lead a child with ADHD to lose focus, become distracted, and therefore become disruptive to your class.

- **Be more animated, theatrical, and dramatic when you teach** (make it interesting!). Be like Robin Williams in the movie, *The Dead Poets Society,* not like Ben Stein in *Ferris Bueller's Day Off.* If you are not enthusiastic or interested in what you are teaching, then don't expect the student with ADHD to be interested in it.

- **Touch a child lightly when talking to him to get his undivided attention**. This also signals to the child that what you are about to say is important. So when you have something to say to the student with ADHD, go to him, place your hand on his hand, arm, or shoulder, and say what you need to say. But keep it brief – get to the point quickly or you will lose his attention.

- Schedule the **most difficult subjects in the first few periods** of the school day when the student's attention span is at its maximum. Leave the more active and entertaining subjects for a later time of the day.

- Use direct instruction, programmed learning, or highly structured or regimented teaching materials that have **short assignments, clear goals, and frequent quizzes** to provide feedback to the ADHD student for demonstrating mastery of the material.

- Have the child **prestate her work goals**. Ask her, "How many problems can you do for me in the next 5 minutes?" A child with ADHD are more likely to do an assignment she has chosen than one imposed on her by another. After she completes it, if you want more work done, then ask her how many more problems she can do for you. Again, the concept here is to give brief periods of work interspersed with brief breaks so as to refresh the student's short attention span.

Train the student in **keyboarding and word processor skills as early as possible**. This is because students with ADHD have a high occurrence of fine motor coordination problems and difficulties with handwriting. So don't tax their deficits in motor control so much and give them alternative means of expressing their ideas in print.

Give the student with ADHD **after-school help sessions, extra tutoring, books on tape, and videos** to reinforce the class work you have assigned. When he stays after school to meet with you, you can then assist him with homework completion.

**Require continuous note taking** during class and while the child is reading assigned material. The child with ADHD should be taking brief notes of key points in what she is reading, viewing, or listening so as to help focus and sustain her attention to the work. Again, permit some movement while she is concentrating. This not only reduces ADHD symptoms but it can help to improve her poor working memory.

Suggest to parents that they consider **combining the behavioral interventions discussed** throughout this book with ADHD medications to maximize the benefits of both.

# Peer Tutoring

Evidence clearly demonstrates that when students with ADHD work in dyads with their peers in order to learn new material, they are more likely to concentrate and to learn that material more quickly than if they just listen to a classroom lecture. This is known as peer tutoring. It essentially involves the following brief steps:

1. Create, discuss, and distribute scripts (worksheets based on the concept or skill you are teaching).

2. Teach any new concepts and skills to class as you normally would do so.

3. Provide initial instructions for work that is to be done.

4. Now break the class up into dyads (pairs).

5. Have one student be the tutor. That student is to teach the other student in the pair what it was the teacher just taught during the lecture and that is contained on the worksheet. This student-tutor then quizzes her partner on the material.

6. You should move around or circulate in the classroom during this time, supervise behavior, and coach the dyads as needed.

7. Be sure to alternate who plays the tutor/student roles in the dyad for the next task or assignment.

8. Reorganize the class into new dyads daily or weekly so that the same children are not working together in the same pair for too long.

9. Graph or post quiz results on a bulletin board at the front of the class.

# CHAPTER 8

# Increase Rewards
# for Good Behavior

As noted in Chapter 2, students with ADHD have far less self-motivation than do other students. This means they will not be able to persist as long as others in doing work for which there are no immediate rewards or consequences more generally. To help make up for this intrinsic motivation deficit, teachers need to provide more "external" or artificial consequences to students with ADHD when work is to be done. Numerous approaches can be used:

🖊 **Increase your use of verbal praise, approval, appreciation**, and other forms of positive feedback for the ADHD student's good behavior and work performance.

🖊 **Be a 1-minute manager** (lots of short episodes of praise throughout the class period). For several decades, one of the best-selling business management books has been *The One Minute Manager* by Kenneth H. Blanchard.

   The essence of this book was that the best managers who had the best relations with employees and received the most work from those employees were those who did the following: They spent only as much time in their office as was essential to do. They spent far more time periodically circulating among their staff. When they did, they would just take 1 minute with an employee, notice anything good, useful, productive, or otherwise positive that the employee had done, comment briefly on it and how much that work was appreciated, and in other ways show that they valued this employee. They make sure that the comments are accurate statements of what the employee has done and that the appreciation being shown is realistic.

   Excessive and cloying praise will not be well received, but brief, accurate statements of recognition for work well done and realistic appreciation for that work will be well-accepted and result in greater future motivation by this employee to contribute further to workplace productivity. Then a supervisor would move on to another employee and do the same. Teachers should do the same with their students, but especially with those students with ADHD.

🖊 **Use a token or point system to organize privileges and their price**. Token economy management systems provide students with "tokens," known as secondary reinforcers, when students demonstrate a specific target behavior.

41

# Token Economy Reinforcement System

1. Determine the goals to be met (for example, completion of independent seat-work).

2. Choose the type of token to be used (for example, poker chips, stickers, checkmarks on a card at the student's desk).

3. Decide how many tokens are to be earned for demonstrating each particular target behavior (teachers can break more complex tasks down into component parts and give tokens for each part completed).

4. Student and teacher work out the types of activities and other privileges that the tokens could be exchanged for (for example, five tokens equals five minutes of free time at a classroom computer or iPad). Create a written menu of these activities and their associated costs and post this menu in a visible place near the student.

5. Students are taught the value of the tokens (model what has to happen to earn a token and explain what the tokens can be exchanged for within the available classroom toys, games, and other activities).

6. Students can exchange tokens for activities on a daily basis. Don't delay the exchange beyond a day. And the more frequent the exchange takes place during the day, the more motivating the tokens are likely to be.

7. The intervention should be monitored to assess its effectiveness — Does it work? Are there increases in appropriate target behaviors?

Teachers have limited or no budgets for buying **toys, games, computers, and other privileges for their classroom**. To address this problem, ask parents to send in old games/toys to upgrade the class supply of fun activities. You can do this at the beginning of the school year by sending home a memo to parents asking them to clean out their closets, cabinets, and basements of any older toys that their child no longer uses.

Instead of donating these to Goodwill Stores, as parents often do, give them to the school. These donations are tax deductible, just like at Goodwill. Send the memo out again after the Christmas school break, and you are likely to get another load of toys, games, and so on to help bolster the available rewards you have in your classroom.

**Get video games donated to the class for use during free time** and make it one of the privileges to be earned through the class point system. Many families have older versions of Game Boy, X-Box, PlayStation, and other gaming devices that their children may no longer be using, having upgraded to the latest models. But these videogames are still fun to play and can be motivating to other students in the classroom as rewards for getting work done and earning the necessary tokens to get that privilege.

🖊 **Team-based (group) activities and associated rewards**. This approach capitalizes on the fun of team competition to learn and get work done. Divide your class into teams of 4–5 students per team. The members of the teams are to work together to complete a project or assignment. The teams compete against other teams in getting work done and striving to earn tokens or other rewarding activities. Team members are likely to help keep each other focused and on task and provide beneficial structure and encouragement to the student with ADHD on that team.

🖊 Try creating (or buying) **a tone-tape for use with a self-reward program** (you can buy these recordings at addwarehouse.com) as described below:
- Create an audio digital recording that is composed of tones, such as a bell ringing, a buzzer sounding, a piano key, or any other sound. These sounds are recorded so that the time gaps between them are unpredictable. This creates a variable interval frequency schedule of tones. For the first recording, make the tones occur frequently but keep the brief intervals between the tones unpredictable or random.
- This recording is to be used when students have work to do at their desks.
- When you are ready to use this recording, tell the class that you are turning on a recording of some sounds. They will hear these sounds while they are working. Now, when a tone sounds while they are doing desk work, the students are to self-evaluate by asking themselves if they were working (on task) or not when the sound was heard.

  If so, the students are to then give themselves a point if they were working when the tone sounded. If they were off task, they must deduct a point from their scorecards. Students can use + and − signs on the card to indicate this. When the work is completed, the students can add up how many tokens they earned (pluses), which is how many they have to spend on various activities in the token system discussed earlier.

🖊 **Use the Attention Training System** – this is a small, automated box for dispensing frequent rewards to ADHD children during work periods. The box has a digital display panel on the front that shows how many points a student has earned. There is a red light on the top of the box and a buzzer inside the box. When the student starts working at their desk, the device is turned on. The box will give the student a point per minute.

The teacher carries a small wireless transmitter. If she sees the student off-task or otherwise not working, she presses a button on this transmitter. A red light flashes on the box, the buzzer sounds, and a point is subtracted from the total points shown on the digital display. In short, the box delivers the rewards at a frequent pace while the teacher periodically removes points if the student gets off-task. After the work period ends, the student can use these points to buy privileges in the classroom token system.

⬗ Regardless of what type of token system is established, you should **allow students access to the rewards of the classroom often** (daily or more often) and not at the end of the school week. The longer you delay letting students exchange their tokens for privileges, the less valuable the tokens will be in motivating appropriate behavior.

⬗ **Tokens can also be taken back when a student engages in inappropriate behavior or is off-task**. This is known as response cost. If you do this, be sure to keep the ratio of rewards to punishments at 2:1 or greater. This way, students are always earning more tokens than they are losing. You want your class token system to remain a rewarding, not a punitive one. If the ratio drops to 1:1, so that students are losing as many points as they earn, or has students going into debt (the red) with more fines than they have tokens accumulated, the system will no longer work to motivate students to behave well and work appropriately.

# CHAPTER 9

# Daily Behavior Report Cards and Behavior Contracts

Two of the most effective tools for helping to improve the behavior and school performance of children with ADHD are daily behavior report cards, also known as note-home cards, and behavior contracts. Both are examples of proactive teaching and behavior management rather than the customary reactive approach many teachers take with ADHD students. Here, a plan is set up in advance of any problem occurrence and in order to ward off the likelihood of such problems arising. It also increases the probability that appropriate behavior and school performance will occur instead.

## Creating Daily Behavior Report Cards

Any behavior recording system, or report card, must be set up according to certain rules if it is to be maximally effective.

- Daily goals must be stated in positive manner.
- The card specifies both behavioral and academic goals.
- The targets are to be a small number of goals.
- The teacher provides quantitative feedback – usually a numerical rating or grade.
- The feedback is provided at the end of each class period.
- There is to be regular daily communication with parents (the card goes home each school day for review by the parents).
- Consequences are established at home and are tied to the student's school behavior and performance. Parents essentially set up a home token system in which a list of privileges is created and a point value or cost is assigned to each. The tokens or points earned from the daily report cards are to be spent for these privileges.
- Solicit parental cooperation before starting.
- Get student input into the goals especially for older children and teens.
- Review the card weekly for any necessary modifications.

The following handout contains the instructions that can be shared with parents about a daily behavior report card, how to implement it, and the kinds of cards teachers and parents can create for use with a student with ADHD.

45

# Parent-Teacher Handout

### Using a Daily School Behavior Report Card

A daily school behavior report card involves having the teacher send home an evaluation of your child's behavior in school that day, which can be used by you to give or take away rewards available at home. These cards have been shown to be effective in modifying a wide range of problems with children at school.

Due to their convenience and cost effectiveness and the fact that they involve both the teacher(s) and parents, they are often one of the first interventions you should try if behavior problems at school are occurring with your child. The teacher reports can consist of either a note or a more formal report card. We recommend the use of a formal behavior report card like those shown at the end of this handout.

The card should list the "target" behavior(s) that are to be the focus of the program on the left-hand side of the card. Across the top should be numbered columns that correspond to each class period at school. The teacher gives a number rating reflecting how well the child did for each of these behaviors for each class period. Some examples are provided at the end of this chapter.

### How the Daily Report Card Works

Using this system, teacher reports are typically sent home on a daily basis. As the child's behavior improves, the daily reports can be reduced to twice weekly (Wednesdays and Fridays), once weekly, or even monthly, and finally phased out altogether. A variety of daily report cards may be developed and tailored for your child.

Some of the behaviors targeted for the program may include both social conduct (shares, plays well with peers, follows rules) and academic performance (completes math or reading assignments). Targeting low academic performance (poor production of work) may be especially effective.

Examples of behaviors to target include completing all (or a specified portion of) work, staying in the assigned seat, following teacher directions, and playing cooperatively with others. Negative behaviors (e.g., aggression, destruction, calling out) may also be included as target behaviors to be reduced by the program. In addition to targeting class performance, homework may be included.

Children sometimes have difficulty remembering to bring homework assignments home. They may also complete their homework but forget to return the completed work to school the next day. Each of these areas may be targeted in a school behavior report card program.

It is recommended that the number of target behaviors you work on be kept to about four or five. Start out by focusing on just a few behaviors you wish to change, to help maximize your child's success in the program. When these behaviors are going well, you can add a few more problem behaviors as targets for change. We recommend including at least one or two positive behaviors that the child is currently doing well with, so that the child will be able to earn some points during the beginning of the program.

Typically, children are monitored throughout the school day. However, to be successful with problem behaviors that occur very frequently, you may want to have the child initially rated for only a portion of the school day, such as for one or two subjects or classes. As the child's behavior improves, the card can be expanded gradually to include more periods/subjects until the child is being monitored throughout the day. In cases where children attend several different classes taught by different teachers, the program may involve some or all of the teachers, depending on the need for help in each of the classes. When more than one teacher is included in the program, a single report card may include space for all teachers to rate the child.

Alternatively, different report cards may be used for each class and organized in a notebook for children to carry between classes. Again, the card shown at the end of this handout can be helpful because it has columns that can be used to rate the child by the same teacher at the end of each subject, or by different teachers.

The success of the program depends on a clear, consistent method for translating the teacher's reports into consequences at home. One advantage of school behavior report cards is that a wide variety of consequences can be used. At a minimum, praise and positive attention should be provided at home whenever a child does well that day at school, as shown on the report card.

With many children, however, tangible rewards or token programs are often necessary. For example, a positive note home may translate into television time, a special snack, or a later bedtime. A token system may also be used in which a child earns points for positive behavior ratings and loses points for negative ratings. Both daily rewards (e.g., time with parent, special dessert, television time) and weekly rewards (e.g., movie, dinner at a restaurant, special outing) may be included in the program.

### Advantages of the Daily Report Card

Overall, daily school behavior report cards can be as or even more effective than classroom-based behavior management programs, with effectiveness increased when combined with classroom-based programs.

Daily reports seem particularly well suited for children because the children often benefit from the more frequent feedback than is usually provided at school. These programs also give parents more frequent feedback than would normally be provided by the child. As you know, most children, when asked how their school day went, give you a one-word answer, "Fine," which may not be accurate.

These report card programs also can remind parents when to reward a child's behavior, and forewarn parents when behavior is becoming a problem at school and will require more intensive work. In addition, the type and quality of rewards available in the home are usually far more extensive than those available in the classroom, a factor that may be critical with children who need more powerful rewards.

Aside from these benefits, daily school report cards generally require much less time and effort from your child's teacher than do classroom-based programs. As a result, teachers who have been unable to start a classroom management program may be far more likely to cooperate with a daily report card that comes from home.

Despite the impressive success of report card programs, the effectiveness of the program depends on the teacher accurately evaluating the child's behavior. It also hinges on the fair and consistent use of consequences at home.

In some cases, children may attempt to undercut the system by failing to bring home a report. They may forge a teacher's signature or fail to get a certain teacher's signature. To discourage these practices, missing notes or signatures should be treated the same way as a "bad" report (i.e., child fails to earn points or is fined by losing privileges or points). The child may even be grounded for the day (no privileges) for not bringing the card home.

### Some Examples of Daily School Report Cards

Several types of school behavior report cards that rely on daily school behavior ratings will be discussed here. Two examples are provided at the end of this handout. These are the cards we recommend most parents use if they want to start a school behavior report card quickly.

One card is for classroom behavior, the other is for recess behavior. Use whichever card is most appropriate for the problems your child is having at school.

Notice that each card contains five areas of potential behavior problems that children may experience. For the class behavior report card, columns are provided for up to seven different teachers to rate the child in these areas of behavior or for one teacher to rate the child many times across the school day.

We have found that the more frequent the ratings, the more effective is the feedback for the children and the more informative the program is to you. The teacher initials the bottom of the column after rating the child's performance during that class period to ensure against forgery. If getting the correct homework assignment home is a problem for some children, the teacher can require the child to copy the homework for that class period on the back of the card before completing the ratings for that period.

In this way, the teacher merely checks the back of the card for the child's accuracy in copying the assignment and then completes the ratings on the front of the card. For particularly negative ratings, we also encourage teachers to provide a brief explanation to you as to what resulted in that negative mark. The teachers rate the children using a 5-point system (1 = excellent, 2 = good, 3 = fair, 4 = poor, and 5 = very poor).

The child takes a new card to school each day. These can be kept at school and a new card given out each morning, or you can provide the card as your child leaves for school, whichever is most likely to be done consistently. As soon as the child returns home, you should immediately inspect the card, discuss the positive ratings first with your child, and then proceed to a neutral, businesslike (not angry!) discussion with your child about any negative marks and the reason for them. Your child should then be asked to formulate a plan for how to avoid getting a negative mark tomorrow. You are to remind your child of this plan the next morning before your child departs for school. After the child formulates the plan, you should award your child points for each rating on the card and deduct points for each negative mark.

For instance, a young elementary school-aged child may receive five chips for a 1, three for a 2, and one chip for a 3, while being fined three chips for a 4 and five chips for a 5 on the card. For older children, the points might be 25, 15, 5, −15, and −25, respectively, for marks 1–5 on the card. The chips or points are then added up, the fines are subtracted, and the child may then spend what is left of these chips on the privileges on the home reward menu.

Another daily report card program is provided for dealing with behavior problems and getting along with others during school recess periods or free time periods each day. The card is to be completed by the teacher on recess duty during each recess or free time period. It is inspected by the class teacher when the child returns to the classroom, and then should be sent home for use, as above, in a home chip/point system. The classroom teacher should also be instructed to use a "think aloud–think ahead" procedure with the child just prior to the child's going out for recess or free time. In this procedure, the teacher (1) reviews the rules for proper recess behavior with the child and notes that they are written on the card, (2) reminds the child that he/she is being watched by the teacher on recess duty, and (3) directs the child to give the card immediately to the recess monitor so the monitor can evaluate the child's behavior during recess or free time.

As these cards illustrate, virtually any child behavior can be the target for treatment using behavior report cards. If the cards shown here are not suited for your child's behavior problems at school, then design a new card using the blank cards provided. They do not take long to construct and can be very helpful in improving a child's school behavior and performance.

---

**For your convenience, you may download the following report cards at go.pesi.com/barkley**

## SAMPLE — Daily School Behavior Report Card

Child's name **Joe Smith**

Teacher: **Ms. Swanson**     Date **Jan. 1st**

Please rate this child's behavior today in the areas listed below. Use a separate column for each subject or class period. Use the following ratings:
1 = excellent, 2 = good, 3 = fair, 4 = poor, and 5 = very poor. Then initial the box at the bottom of your column. Add any comments about the child's behavior today on the back of this card.

| Behaviors to be rated: | Class periods/subjects | | | | | | |
|---|---|---|---|---|---|---|---|
| | ① | ② | ③ | ④ | ⑤ | ⑥ | ⑦ |
| Class participation | 3 | 3 | 2 | 3 | 2 | 2 | 3 |
| Performance of class work | 2 | 4 | 3 | 3 | 2 | 3 | 3 |
| Follows classroom rules | 4 | 2 | 2 | 4 | 3 | 4 | 3 |
| Gets along well with other children | 3 | 3 | 4 | 3 | 2 | 5 | 4 |
| Quality of homework, if any given | 2 | 2 | 2 | 3 | 3 | 3 | 3 |
| Teacher's initials | MS | HO | KM | MO | LJ | MG | EK |
| Place comments below or on back of card. | Joe had trouble today following the quiet time rule. MS | | | | | | |

# Daily School Behavior Report Card

Child's name _____ Date _____

Teacher: _____

Please rate this child's behavior today in the areas listed below. Use a separate column for each subject or class period. Use the following ratings:
1 = excellent, 2 = good, 3 = fair, 4 = poor, and 5 = very poor. Then initial the box at the bottom of your column. Add any comments about the child's behavior today on the back of this card.

| Behaviors to be rated: | Class periods/subjects | | | | | | |
|---|---|---|---|---|---|---|---|
| | ① | ② | ③ | ④ | ⑤ | ⑥ | ⑦ |
| Class participation | | | | | | | |
| Performance of class work | | | | | | | |
| Follows classroom rules | | | | | | | |
| Gets along well with other children | | | | | | | |
| Quality of homework, if any given | | | | | | | |
| Teacher's initials | | | | | | | |
| Place comments below or on back of card. | | | | | | | |

From *Defiant Children*. Copyright 1997 by The Guilford Press. Reprinted with permission.

# Daily School Behavior Report Card

Child's name _____ Date _____

Teacher: _____

Please rate this child's behavior today in the areas listed below. Use a separate column for each subject or class period. Use the following ratings:
1 = excellent, 2 = good, 3 = fair, 4 = poor, and 5 = very poor. Then initial the box at the bottom of your column. Add any comments about the child's behavior today on the back of this card.

| Behaviors to be rated: | Class periods/subjects | | | | | | |
|---|---|---|---|---|---|---|---|
| | ① | ② | ③ | ④ | ⑤ | ⑥ | ⑦ |
| | | | | | | | |
| | | | | | | | |
| | | | | | | | |
| | | | | | | | |
| | | | | | | | |
| | | | | | | | |
| | | | | | | | |

# SAMPLE — Daily Recess and Free Time Behavior Report Card

Child's name __Joe Smith__

Teacher: __Ms. Swanson__   Date __Jan. 1st__

Please rate this child's behavior today during recess or other free time periods in the areas listed below. Use a separate column for each recess/ free time period. Use the following ratings: 1 = excellent, 2 = good, 3 = fair, 4 = poor, and 5 = very poor. Then initial at the bottom of the column. Add any comments on the back.

| Behaviors to be rated: | Class periods/subjects | | | | | | |
|---|---|---|---|---|---|---|---|
| | ① | ② | ③ | ④ | ⑤ | ⑥ | ⑦ |
| Keeps hands to self; does not push, shove | 3 | 3 | 3 | 3 | 2 | 2 | 3 |
| Does not tease others | 4 | 3 | 4 | 4 | 3 | 4 | 2 |
| Follows recess/free time rules | 2 | 2 | 2 | 2 | 3 | 3 | 3 |
| Gets along well with other children | 2 | 3 | 2 | 3 | 3 | 2 | 3 |
| Does not fight or hit | 2 | 3 | 3 | 2 | 2 | 3 | 2 |
| Teacher's initials | MS | HO | KM | MO | LJ | MG | EK |
| Place comments below or on back of card. | Joe was teasing Brooke today about her new haircut. MS | | | | | | |

From *Defiant Children*. Copyright 1997 by The Guilford Press. Reprinted with permission.

# Daily Recess and Free Time Behavior Report Card

Child's name _____ Date _____

Teacher: _____

Please rate this child's behavior today during recess or other free time periods in the areas listed below. Use a separate column for each recess/ free time period. Use the following ratings: 1 = excellent, 2 = good, 3 = fair, 4 = poor, and 5 = very poor. Then initial at the bottom of the column. Add any comments on the back.

| Behaviors to be rated: | Class periods/subjects | | | | | | |
|---|---|---|---|---|---|---|---|
| | ① | ② | ③ | ④ | ⑤ | ⑥ | ⑦ |
| Keeps hands to self; does not push, shove | | | | | | | |
| Does not tease others | | | | | | | |
| Follows recess/free time rules | | | | | | | |
| Gets along well with other children | | | | | | | |
| Does not fight or hit | | | | | | | |
| Teacher's initials | | | | | | | |
| Place comments below or on back of card. | | | | | | | |

From *Defiant Children*. Copyright 1997 by The Guilford Press. Reprinted with permission.

# Daily Recess and Free Time Behavior Report Card

Child's name _____ Date _____

Teacher: _____

Please rate this child's behavior today during recess or other free time periods in the areas listed below. Use a separate column for each recess/ free time period. Use the following ratings: 1 = excellent, 2 = good, 3 = fair, 4 = poor, and 5 = very poor. Then initial at the bottom of the column. Add any comments on the back.

| Behaviors to be rated: | Class periods/subjects | | | | | | |
|---|---|---|---|---|---|---|---|
| | ① | ② | ③ | ④ | ⑤ | ⑥ | ⑦ |
| | | | | | | | |
| | | | | | | | |
| | | | | | | | |
| | | | | | | | |
| | | | | | | | |
| | | | | | | | |

# Behavioral Contracting

Instead of a behavior report card, teachers can set up an in-class behavior contract. These contracts should contain the following elements.

1. **Set academic work and behavioral goals explicitly and clearly in a written form**, for instance:
   - I (the student) agree to complete all of my written math and language arts work with at least 80 percent accuracy.
   - I will remain quiet, follow directions, and listen.

2. **Specify rewards to be earned explicitly**, for example:
   - 15 extra minutes of playtime at end of school day
   - Access to special "reserved" toys or play activities
   - Use of class computer for play or work for 15 extra minutes
   - 10 points for every task completed accurately
   - Helping teacher by completing some errands or in-class jobs
   - If I have a successful week, I will earn a special activity with my parents.

3. **Specify punishment explicitly**, for example:
   - Loss of 10 points or tokens for each task not completed
   - 5 sheets of "do a task" in time out

It is helpful to have the student sign the contract and for a copy of the contract to be posted in a visible location near the student so he or she can make reference to it throughout the class period.

# CHAPTER 10
# Externalize Information and Time

Recall from Chapter 2 that children and teens with ADHD have poor working memory. That means they cannot hold as much information in mind or for as long as other students. They are also less likely to call up such information from memory and keep it consciously in mind when they are entering class periods or a change in a situation from a prior activity to the next or new one.

Because "internal" or mental information is not especially effective at guiding an ADHD student's behavior, it is helpful to boost working memory by placing key pieces of information in the student's visual or other sensory fields in that work location. I call putting such information in a physical form in the visual field of the student "externalizing" the key information and cues.

This chapter briefly reviews some ways that teachers can help "externalize" critical pieces of information about the situation and any time intervals that may be important for that situation, class, or work period. This is another example of a form of proactive teaching and behavior management rather than the customary reactive approach. Here, a plan is set up in advance of any problem occurrence in order to ward off the likelihood of such problems arising. The methods lessen the likelihood that problems will occur and increase the likelihood that a student will behave appropriate and work effectively in that situation.

## Make Rules Obvious and in Physical Forms

🖊 **Post rules on posters at the front of the class –** you can post different sets of rules for each type of work period.

# Classroom Rules

## 1. Listening Bodies
(I will listen and follow Directions.)

## 2. Raised Hands
(I will raise my hand to share ideas)

## 3. Quiet Mouths
(I will use a soft voice.)

*▨* **Create a three-sided stop sign from poster board**. Each side is a different color and each contains the rules for one of three different situations. For instance, use:
- Red = lecture time, yellow = desk work, green = free play
- When the new situation starts, call the class to attention, then rotate the sign to the appropriate color and rules for the appropriate situation, then have students read these rules out loud in unison.

*▨* **Place laminated color-coded card sets on the student's desk** such that each card contains a set of rules for each subject or class activity. When that activity starts, direct students to turn their card deck to the appropriate set of rules for that activity. Each activity has different rules and a different color card to make it easier to identify. Have the child state the rules on that card at the start of each activity.

Encourage the child to use **soft vocal self-instruction during work**. The child talks to herself periodically while working, saying out loud in a soft voice the instructions she is to follow. Or, she can softly read aloud the rules on the card for that work period, as discussed previously.

*▨* Make sure you are giving your commands and **instructions to a child in an effective manner**. Here are some key points to keep in mind to help you do so:
- *Make sure you mean it!* That is, never give a command that you do not intend to see followed through to its completion. When you make a request, plan on backing it up with appropriate consequences, either positive or negative, to show that you mean what you have said.
- *Do not present the command as a question or favor.* State the command simply, directly, and in a businesslike tone of voice.
- *Do not give too many commands at once.* Most children are able to follow only one or two instructions at a time. For now, try giving only one specific instruction at a time. If a task you want your child to do is complicated, then break it down into smaller steps and give only one step at a time.
- *Make sure the child is paying attention to you.* Be sure that you have eye contact with the child. If necessary, go to the child, touch his shoulder, or gently turn the child's face toward yours to ensure that he is listening and watching when the command is given.
- *Reduce all distractions before giving the command.* This is a common mistake that teachers make. Often, teachers try to give instructions while a student is engaged in some competing activity, usually something fun. You cannot expect children to attend to you when something more entertaining is going on in the room. Either turn off or terminate these distractions yourself or tell the child to turn them off before giving the command.
- *Ask the child to repeat the command.* This need not be done with each request, but can be done if you are not sure the child heard or understood the command. Also, for children with a short attention span, having them repeat the command appears to increase the likelihood they will follow it through.

- *Make up task cards.* If your student is old enough to have tasks to do about the classroom, then you may find it useful to make up a chore or task card for each job. Or, as noted earlier, you can make up cards containing the rules for particular subjects you are teaching, such as reading time, math time, and so on. Each card can be a different color to further signal that the rules during this subject are different from those for other subjects.

This subject card or task card can simply be a 3 × 5 file card. Listed on it are the steps involved in correctly doing that task or for that subject period. Then, when the child is to begin that task or subject, simply hand the child the card and state that this is what you want done. This is only for children who are old enough to read.

These cards can greatly reduce the amount of arguing that occurs about whether a child has done a job or chore properly or obeyed the rules for a particular class period. You might also indicate on the card how much time the task should take to complete and then set a kitchen timer for this time period and place it on the child's desk or at her workstation so she knows exactly when it is to be done.

✏ **Create "nag tapes"** – a digitally recorded set of encouragements recorded by Dad or Mom (or the teacher) with reminders of the rules for on-task behavior. The child can listen to this recording using ear buds during schoolwork.

## Make Time Real (Physical)

Children and teens with ADHD cannot manage or guide their behavior based on their sense of time, and teachers should not rely so much on a child's subjective sense of time, which is impaired in children with ADHD. The goal then is to "externalize" time, which essentially means using some external time-keeping device to help the children with ADHD to see how much time they have to do something, and then how much of it has passed and how much is left in the assigned time period as they complete their work.

To do this, you can use clocks, timers, watches, or recorded time signals, anything to show how much time they have to do an assignment. For example, you can use the Time Timer, which is a timer device that is an 8 inch x 8 inch clock with a red dial on it that signals a time period for up to one hour. When a child has deskwork to do within a set time period, you can set this clock to that time period. The time available shows up in red on the clock face and as time passes, the amount of red exposed decreases until time us up and a signal sounds to indicate the end of the work period. Digital timers can also be found on the Internet, such as the My Time Activity Timer.

You can also download a variety of online stopwatches and timer apps for a tablet, iPad, or smartphone at http://www.online-stopwatch.com/classroom-timers/. These include traditional clock faces, time bombs, cartoon characters running races, virtual hourglasses, and so on.

## CHAPTER 11

# Improving Self-Awareness

Children and teens with ADHD are less aware of their own behavior than are typical students because they do not monitor their ongoing behavior as well or as often as do other students. Research does not show any definitive means by which teachers can improve the self-awareness or self-monitoring of students with ADHD. However, here are some methods that have been used by clinical researchers and others:

✏ **Have the child record his work productivity on a daily chart or graph.** Put this graph on public display, such as on a bulletin board at the front of the class. Each day the student records how many problems he completed in a particular class period on this graph or chart. This is done so the student can see how well he is performing in class over time.

✏ Go back and look at the **daily behavior report cards** in Chapter 9. You can easily see that these could be cards that are completed by the child instead of the teacher at the end of each class period. In other words, the child provides a self-evaluation of her behavior and performance in the areas specified on the card. This can be done using the same rating scale that the teacher was using to rate or grade the child's behavior.

The child rates herself on this daily conduct card and the teacher checks it to see if he/she agrees with the child's self-evaluation. If not, the teacher discusses this difference of opinion and any reasons for disagreeing with the child. Then the child can re-rate the card based on this new feedback. I encourage teachers to start with a standard behavior report card that they complete. Then, after a few weeks when the child's behavior seems to have improved, the teacher can transition over to this type of self-evaluation.

For young children, researchers have developed **a simpler cueing system** for letting children know that they may be behaving inappropriately and to stop and self-monitor their current actions. For instance, the teacher cues a young child to immediately stop and self-monitor by saying the word "Turtle." The child has been previously instructed that when he hears the teacher say that word to him, he is to:

1. Stop what he is doing, pull in his hands and arms to his sides, and legs close together.
2. Slowly look about the classroom to regain his sense of where he is and what is happening.
3. The child asks himself out loud, "What was I told to do?"
4. Then the child is to give the answer and return to the assigned task, or follow the instruction that he was given.
5. For successfully doing so, some teachers have given children small ink-stamp impressions on their hand using an ink-stamp containing the picture of a turtle. The children collect these stamps on the back of their hand throughout the day. These turtle stamps then are used like tokens to purchase special privileges in class later that day. Or the teacher can substitute turtle stickers that are glued to a card kept on the children's desk. If those sorts of stickers cannot be purchased, then the teacher can simply give the student a token, like a poker chip, for each successful act of self-monitoring.

Use **a device called the Motivaider**, which is a vibrating small box with a built-in digital timer. This small box is worn by the child on a belt or placed in a pocket. It is a tactile cueing device that vibrates at intervals set by the teacher. These intervals can be fixed (e.g., every minute) or they can be random, based on the setting chosen. The timer then periodically cues the child with a vibration stimulus, which means to self-monitor what they are doing or to pay attention to the assigned work.

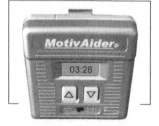

For older children or teens with ADHD, I have recommended the use of **nonverbal confidential cues to signal to them to stop and self-monitor** their current actions. You can do this by telling the teen beforehand that when she sees you show this signal, she is to self-evaluate what she is doing and get back to work, get back to following a given instruction, or just settle down and regain behavioral control if that is the issue. For example, you can say to the student that if you drop a paper clip by her desk, it was no accident. For her, it's a cue to self-evaluate, regain control, or otherwise pay attention to teacher.

In more severe cases of ADHD, you or a school psychologist can consider **video recording the child during a particular troublesome class period**. Afterwards, during a scheduled time for this purpose later that day, the student and you or the psychologist can review the recording with the child, stopping the video periodically to discuss what the child was doing correctly or incorrectly at certain key moments. Then discuss what the child could be doing differently, if a problem was noted. I recommend that this method be paired with some type of reward system, such as a token system, to reward the student for both the review period (when you go over the video together) and for improvements the student subsequently makes in classroom behavior during that period.

# CHAPTER 12

# Transition Planning

Children and teens with ADHD, have trouble not only with working memory (remembering the rules that apply in a given situation) but also with self-monitoring their own behavior. Both of these problems conspire along with their inattentiveness to pose frequent problems during times when students are transitioning from one activity, class period, or classroom to the next. As a result, problem behaviors can often occur during or just after such transitions. To help address this situation, I recommend developing a method called transition planning. This is to be discussed with the child before it is put into use.

---

**Transition Planning**

In transition planning, BEFORE starting a new activity, class subject, or even entering a new classroom, a student should do the following:

1. Just before entering a new situation (next class, recess, going to lunch room), the teacher asks the child to STOP!

2. The teacher then reviews two to three rules the child needs to obey in this new situation.

3. The child then repeats those rules out loud to the teacher.

4. The teacher explains what the incentive or reward is in that situation for obeying those rules (tokens, time on the computer, extra play time, etc.).

5. The teacher then establishes with the child what the punishment is if a rule is broken.

6. The teacher then assigns the child an immediate instruction to do or activity to start. For instance, the teacher can say, "Go to your desk, get out your math book, and turn to chapter X and start reading."

7. The child then enters the new situation and follows the teacher's plan.

8. The teacher is to reward the student frequently throughout the new activity.

9. At the end of that situation, the teacher speaks briefly with the student to evaluate success (or failure).

---

A teacher can also augment or replace this procedure with a 3 × 5 inch file card on which are written the rules the child is to follow routinely when entering this new situation, class subject, or classroom. That way, the child has the "externalized" rules written on the card to take with him to keep in view on his desk throughout the period.

This is yet another example of a form of proactive teaching and behavior management rather than the customary reactive approach often used with ADHD students. Here, a plan is set up in advance of any problem occurrence in order to ward off the likelihood of such problems arising. Usually, teachers allow students to go through these transitions unassisted. And then when problems develop, the teachers are forced to react to this situation, usually with discipline. Proactive behavior management is far superior to reactive management in creating a better day for both the student with ADHD and the teacher.

# CHAPTER 13

# Discipline

Before implementing any of the disciplinary ideas or methods listed here, a teacher should check with the school principal or district as to policies concerning school guidelines or even regulations pertaining to discipline or punishment. The following are some methods I and others have previously implemented in schools as forms of punishment for student misbehavior:

🖊 **Use mild, private, brief, direct reprimands** – personalize that information. That means, go to the child, touch him on the arm or shoulder, make a brief corrective statement or instruction, and have the student repeat it back. Direct, personalized instructions or reprimands are far more effective that anonymous ones given to a class as a whole or ones yelled across a room at a student.

🖊 **Immediacy is the key to discipline: Swift justice!** What makes punishment work is not so much its severity, the degree of pain, or unpleasantness afflicted, but the speed with which it is implemented following some misbehavior. By acting quickly following the initial occurrence of a problem you build credibility and will be far more effective in reducing the next occurrence of the same or similar misbehavior.

---

### Steps for the
### "Do A Task" Method

Instead of traditional time out, try the "Do a Task" procedure. In place of the ADHD student sitting idly in a time-out chair, which is an invitation to boredom and further misbehavior, this procedure gives the student something active to be done during time-out. It also lets the child have some control over the length of the time-out by how quickly he gets the task done. All of this needs to be explained to the student beforehand so he understands what you are about to do.

1. Place a vacant desk and chair at the back of the classroom with simple worksheets stacked on it.

2. When a child misbehaves, tell her what she did wrong and give her a number (e.g., you yelled out in class, give me 2).

3. The child then goes to the desk at the back of the class, takes a seat, and does that number of worksheets as part of being timed out.

4. When that work is done, the student places it on the teacher's desk and returns to her normal seat.

---

**Response cost** simply involves a loss of tokens or a privilege contingent on the student's misbehavior. As I warned earlier, however, don't get carried away with this sort of punishment or it will ruin any incentive programs you implement. If loss of rewards like this is exceeding earned rewards, the program will lose any motivating value to that student and so become ineffective.

**Moral essays** involve writing an essay concerning a rule infraction and have been used for centuries as a form of discipline in school settings. Have the child write "Why I should not have . . . (e.g., hit other children) and what I should have done instead." Research shows it does work, mainly for older students, but may not be as effective as other methods discussed here.

**Establish a quiet "chill out" location** where an upset or misbehaving child can be sent for a brief period of isolation from the other students. The purpose of this location is to permit the child the time and a place for regaining emotional control when he is upset.

**Use formal time-outs in class or a private room** – If you plan to use a time-out method, remember to institute it swiftly, within seconds of a rule infraction or misbehavior. Be sure the time-out location is within the classroom or in an adjoining private room that can be supervised or observed. Research shows that hallway time-outs don't work.

For more **serious or repeated forms of misconduct**, consider the use of an in-school suspension or even brief placement in a Behavior Disability class.

# CHAPTER 14

# Tips for Teen Management

Some of what follows has already been discussed previously for children with ADHD. But other methods here have been developed specifically for use with teens with ADHD in school settings.

 Consider using an **ADHD medication in combination** with these and any of the previously described methods for teens. These medications are discussed in Chapter 15. If needed, suggest to parents that they consider rewarding the teen a fee per day if need be. Middle school and high school place far higher demands on students with ADHD for self-organization, time management, self-monitoring, and other executive functions in daily life. These stages of education also have the student interacting with more teachers and other school staff and students, often with much less structure and supervision than were provided in elementary school. For all of these reasons, ADHD medication may be needed to help with ADHD symptom control across the school day and to improve school functioning beyond just the behavioral methods reviewed here. The combination of treatments is far more likely to lead to a successful educational experience for the ADHD student than will either approach alone.

 **Find an adult "Coach" or "Mentor"** at school who will give just 15 minutes per day to help the teen. This person provides three accountability checkups of the student across each school day.

---

### The Coaching Method in School

In short, it works like this:

1. The Coach's office is the student's "locker." This is where the teen goes first thing in the morning, at lunch, after school, and even between some classes rather than going to a locker.

2. The Coach schedules a minimum of three 5-minute checkups across each school day.

3. The teen is to go to his Coach at that time for review of the school day, help with staying organized, monitoring homework assignments on an assignment sheet, tracking the student's behavior through a daily behavior report card, and giving the student a motivational pep talk to get through to next checkup.

4. So, at the start of the day, the student checks in with the Coach, gets a new behavior report card, gets a homework assignment recording sheet (if a calendar or day planner is not being used for this purpose), organizes books for the upcoming classes before lunch, and listens to a motivational pep talk.

---

> **5.** At lunch, the teen returns to visit the Coach. The Coach inspects and discusses what is on the behavior report card from the morning's teacher evaluations. The Coach also reviews the homework assignment sheet. And then the Coach helps the student organize needed books and materials for the upcoming classes and gives encouragement for the afternoon classes.
>
> **6.** The student checks in with the Coach at the end of the school day for a review of the behavior report card, the assignment sheet, help with organizing materials that need to go home to do homework, and any further discussion of issues that arose across the day.

Even if a Coach is not being utilized, students with ADHD can still benefit from **using daily assignment sheets for recording homework**.

Teens can also benefit from using a daily or weekly **school behavior card** (see the preceding box). When the student can go for two weeks with no negative ratings, then she can move to using the card as a form of self-evaluation as discussed in an earlier chapter.

**Keep an extra set of books at home** should the student forget the necessary textbooks for a homework assignment that night. Parents can leave a deposit with the school office for these extra books and return them for a refund of that deposit at the end of the year.

Let ADHD teens use **typing/keyboard skills for written assignments** rather than cursive writing, if handwriting is a problem for the teen as it can be for many of them.

Allow the teen to **digitally record lectures** so he can listen to the recording later when studying (check out the Smart Pen at www.livescribe.com for this purpose). The Smart Pen™ is a computer in a pen that helps you never miss a word. The Pulse™ technology recording tablet helps students to record everything they hear, say, and write, and links the audio recordings to their notes. Students can find the most important information from lectures just by tapping on what they wrote. The pen has 2GB of memory and can hold more than 200 hours of audio recording, depending on the settings.

🖊 Ask parents to implement the **"Bucks for Bs"** system: Simply stated, parents pay their teenager for the grades they bring home on any assignment or exam. Teens love money, so this is a great incentive for doing better at school. For instance, for every paper brought home with a grade of C, parents add $.25 to the teen's allowance; for every grade of B, add $.50; and for every A add $1. If they are already paying the teen an allowance, then surely they can realign that allowance with a program like this one to reward improved school work.

🖊 Remember to **schedule harder classes in late morning or early afternoon hours**. Teens are not on the same wake-arousal (diurnal rhythm) cycle as children once the teen enters puberty. Teens are likely to find that they are more alert later in the morning rather than first thing upon arrival at school. So keep this in mind when scheduling classes for a teen with ADHD.

🖊 **Alternate required or difficult classes** with elective or more enjoyable classes across the day where possible.

🖊 **Don't give much, if any, extra time on timed tests** – there is little or no evidence it helps ADHD cases specifically; everyone benefits from a little extra time, such as 10 extra minutes to do a test. But it is better to have a teen with ADHD take the test in a distraction-free test setting and to employ a method called "time off the clock." This involves using a stopwatch placed on the student's desk. The student is permitted the same length of time "on the clock" for testing as other students.

But at any time the student can stop the stopwatch, take a brief break (minute or two of stretching, getting a drink of water, etc.), after which he returns to the test and restarts the stopwatch. The student can do this as often as he feels a need to do so during the test. This will result in extra time being given to that student with ADHD as a by-product of the method. But the granting of extra time is not the solution here or key ingredient. It is the breaking up of the test into shorter chunks of work and letting the teen have frequent breaks and self-pace the exam.

🖊 **Permit teens to listen to music** via ear-buds or earphones at a quiet or reasonable level of volume while doing deskwork, studying, or during homework. Research shows this benefits attention and productivity while working compared to silent study or work periods.

🖉 **Give the teen a written syllabus** as handouts to review and study for each class.

🖉 As noted previously for children, require that the teen with ADHD **engage in note taking** in class and while reading to help her to pay attention.

🖉 Teach the teen **the simple SQ4R** system to boost reading comprehension while studying or doing homework.

---

**The SQ4R Method**

**1.** Survey the assigned material.

**2.** Review or draft questions to be answered, then for each paragraph.

- **Read it.**

- **Recite what is important to remember.**

- **Write it down.**

- **Then review what was written.**

- **Do this again after each new paragraph.**

---

🖉 Try **peer tutoring** in class for teens (page 39).

🖉 **"Study with a buddy"** after school (page 36).

🖉 **Find "fall-back" classmates:** students can swap phone, e-mail, and fax numbers to contact them for lost or missing assignment sheets.

🖉 Require teens to attend **after-school help sessions** whenever available or get some scheduled if not routinely offered to students. If motivation to do so is a problem for the teen with ADHD, see if parents can institute a financial reward for doing so, as in the Bucks for Bs system noted earlier.

🖉 Schedule **parent-teacher review meetings** with the teen every six weeks (but not at a 9-week grading period).

# CHAPTER 15

# Medications Used
# to Manage ADHD

Between 40 and 80 percent of children and teens with ADHD are likely to be taking an ADHD medication as part of their treatment by a physician. It is helpful for educators to know the types of medications their students with ADHD are likely to be taking, how the drugs work, and what the side effects are likely to be. Children taking medication are likely to be more responsive to the behavioral methods used to manage ADHD-related school problems, and the combination of those methods with medication often results in far greater improvement than when either form of treatment is used alone.

## Stimulants and Nonstimulants

Two basic categories of ADHD medicines are approved by the Food and Drug Administration for use with children and teens – *stimulants* and *nonstimulants*. Both have to be taken daily. They all control the symptoms of ADHD only as long as your student takes the medications. They produce no enduring positive effects on your student's ADHD once you stop them. Ceasing the use of medication often results in a return of the ADHD symptoms back to their pretreatment levels. Think of these medicines as you would insulin with a diabetic. Insulin does not cure diabetes, but it does manage it as long as it is used properly for most people. But if your student stops the medication, the underlying problem and its symptoms return.

Both types of ADHD medications typically work by increasing the amount of two (or more) chemicals in the brain known as neurotransmitters. Those chemicals are involved in permitting nerve cells to communicate with each other so the brain can function effectively. More specifically, these drugs increase just how much of these chemicals are residing outside the nerve cells, which can increase the activity of adjacent nerve cells. The two neurotransmitters are dopamine and norepinephrine. By causing nerve cells to express more of these neurochemicals, or by keeping the nerve cells from pulling these chemicals back into the cell once they have been released, they increase the communication that occurs between nerve cells in regions of the brain that are related to directly causing ADHD.

In short, increasing these brain chemicals in these regions lets that brain area function better and sometimes even normally. Also, recent studies show that children who have taken these medications (especially the stimulants) are likely to have brain development that is closer to normal than children with ADHD who have not taken medication – a phenomenon known as *neuroprotection*.

73

## Types of Stimulants and Actions

Two basic types of stimulants are currently marketed in the United States: methylphenidate (MPH) and amphetamine (AMP). These stimulants act in the brain mainly to increase the amount of dopamine available for use outside the nerve cells. Yet they can, to a smaller extent, increase the amount of norepinephrine outside the nerve cells as well. AMP does this mainly by increasing the amount of dopamine that is produced and expressed from the nerve cell when it is activated. To a lesser extent, it may also block the transport system by which the dopamine is normally reabsorbed back into that nerve cell after being released. That can result in more dopamine being left outside the cell to continue to function. MPH mainly acts by preventing much of this reabsorption of dopamine. For this reason, it is known as a transport or reuptake blocker.

Both AMP and MPH have the potential to be abused because they increase dopamine in regions of the brain known as reward centers. Stimulating those centers can lead to an increased likelihood of drug addiction to drugs that do so. But ADHD medications are unlikely to do this when taken by mouth and swallowed, as prescribed. They certainly can do so when they are sniffed through the nose as a powder or injected into a blood vein in a solution, such as when mixed with water. Because of this potential for drug abuse, the U.S. Drug Enforcement Administration has classified the stimulants as Schedule II controlled substances along with other potentially addictive drugs. This classification places limits on how much drug can be produced annually, how the drug is to be prescribed, how it is to be stored in pharmacies, and how it is to be dispensed and otherwise monitored in the United States.

These two drugs are delivered into the body through any one of five methods, which are described in the sidebar. The methods differ in how long they maintain the blood levels of the drug in the body, and so in the brain. Hundreds of studies have been conducted on the safety and effectiveness of these stimulants and delivery systems.

---

### The Five Stimulant Delivery Systems

The five different delivery systems are the 5 Ps – *pills, pumps, pellets, patches, and pro-drug*. The various brand names of ADHD medicines you will hear about are either one form or another of MPH or AMP and involve one of these delivery systems:

#### PILLS

These medicines have been available in this original pill form for many decades. The first versions of AMP were discovered in the 1930s while the first version of MPH was discovered in the 1950s. In pill form, these medications are absorbed quickly, usually within 15–20 minutes, after being taken by mouth and swallowed. They can reach their peak level in the blood (and so in the brain) in 60–90 minutes usually, and may last 3–5 hours in controlling the symptoms of ADHD in most people.

That was their problem. If you wanted to control the symptoms of ADHD across the waking day of say 14–16 hours, you had to give these medications 2–4 times per day or more often. This inconvenience posed to people having to take these drugs is obvious, not to mention the fact that many had to remember to take these drugs so often and frequently forgot to do so.

These and other problems with these immediate-release pills led pharmaceutical companies to explore better ways to get the medicines into the body and keep them active there longer. The brand names you are likely to hear about for these pills are Ritalin® (MPH, a mixture of d-MPH and l-MPH), Focalin® (just d-MPH), Dexedrine® (d-AMP), Benzedrine® (l-AMP), and Adderall® (a mixture of the d- and l-AMP forms or salts).

## THE PUMP

Then came the invention of an ingenious water-pump system for delivering these drugs into the body and keeping them in the blood stream longer. The brand name for this system is Concerta® and it contains MPH. It is a capsule-appearing container with a small laser-drilled hole on one of its long ends. Inside there are two chambers. One chamber contains a paste-like sludge of MPH, and the other chamber is empty. There is also powdered MPH coating the outside of the capsule.

Now here is the neat part: when you swallow the capsule, the powder goes right to work just as it would in the pill form of MPH (i.e., Ritalin), which gives just enough time for the capsule to start to absorb water from your stomach (and later your intestines). The water is absorbed through the wall of the pump in a continuous, even flow into the empty chamber. As that chamber fills up, it presses against the other chamber that contains the MPH paste. That pressure then squeezes the MPH paste out of the hole in the capsule. It is designed to do that continuously for 8–12 hours or more.

The end result is that many people, especially children, only need to take one capsule a day, and not the usual 2–3 (or more) pills they would otherwise have to take. The capsules come in various doses so that physicians can adjust the dose to better suit the individual needs and responses of an ADHD patient.

One problem though is that some older children and teens may need a longer course of medication each day than what this delivery system provides. To deal with that issue, some physicians use the pills of MPH or AMP toward the end of the day. They do this to get an extra 3–5 hours of treatment with medication after the Concerta® may be losing its beneficial control of ADHD symptoms. Even so, you just have to love the human ingenuity that led to the discovery of this delivery system.

## THE PELLETS

At about the same time as the water-pump method was being invented, chemical (pharmacological) engineers were modifying a method that uses time-release pellets as a way to keep medicines in the body and blood stream longer than the pills.

This method had been used for years with some cold medicines, such as the old Contac brand, but the system had to be modified in various ways for use with MPH and AMP. Now we have time-release pellets for both of these stimulants. Little beads of the drug are coated in such a way that some dissolve immediately after being swallowed, others dissolve in 1, 2, 3 or more hours later. This means that the drug can be activated more gradually and absorbed into the blood stream across 8–12 hours for most people.

Here is another ingenious delivery system. It has the added advantage for someone who simply cannot or does not want to swallow the capsule that contains these pellets, of providing the option to open the capsule (pull it apart) and sprinkle the pellets on a teaspoon of applesauce, yogurt, or other food and swallow them that way. It does not change the way the drug will work in the body, typically. You may have heard of these delivery systems by the brand names of Ritalin LA® (MPH), Focalin XR® (d-MPH), Medadate CD® (MPH), and Adderall XR® (AMP) here in the United States.

These capsules come in different doses, which permits a physician to adjust the dose to the optimum level for each individual. Like the water-pump method, these time-release pellet systems sometimes have to be supplemented late in the day with a regular or immediate-release pill version of the same drug. That permits even longer symptom control if necessary.

Some research shows that this pellet system offers slightly better control of ADHD symptoms in the morning than afternoon hours. In contrast, the pump system provides a bit better control in the afternoon than during morning hours. Both delivery systems provide good control of ADHD symptoms across the day but not at exactly the same hours of the day. This can be an issue sometimes in deciding which delivery system may be better for someone depending on when they need the greatest control of their ADHD symptoms during the day.

## THE PATCH

The next invention of a delivery system for the stimulants was FDA-approved just a few years after the pump and the pellet. It is a patch with an adhesive coating that is applied directly to the skin, such as on the back of the shoulder or on the buttocks.

The patch contains MPH. When applied to the skin, the MPH is absorbed through the skin and gets into the blood stream by that means. So long as you wear the patch, MPH is being delivered into the body for as many hours during the day as one wants to do so.

Because the stimulants can cause insomnia or trouble falling asleep, the patch needs to be removed several hours before bedtime to permit the drug left in the body to be broken down and removed without adversely affecting sleep onset.

This delivery system used to go by the brand name Daytrana® (MPH), but the patent on the device is up for sale and may be purchased by another company and renamed in the future.

This is another clever invention for getting the stimulants into the blood stream and keeping them there for a sufficient time to control the symptoms of ADHD across most of the waking day. It has the advantages of not needing to be swallowed and of delivering the medicine into the blood stream as long as you are wearing the patch for that day.

The disadvantage is that you have to remember to take the patch off well before you want to go to sleep. Another problem is that 15–20 percent of people experience a skin rash at the site of the patch and may need to stop using the patch for this reason. As with other forms of the drugs, the patch comes in different doses to better adjust the amount for each individual.

## THE PRO-DRUG

In 2008, another delivery system received FDA approval for use with adults with ADHD, and that system goes by the brand name of Vyvanse® (a form of AMP). Approval came later for using the drug with children and teens. Here is yet a further example of human inventiveness.

One of the problems with the immediate-release pills as well as the pellet systems is that they have the potential to be abused. That is usually done by crushing and inhaling the powder from the pills or the crushed beads from the pellet systems. That powder can also be mixed with water and injected into a blood vein.

Whether snorted through the nose or injected into a vein, the stimulants get into the blood and brain rapidly. This rapid invasion of the brain by the drug and nearly as rapid decrease in certain brain regions are what create the "rush" or euphoria that people can experience with stimulants delivered in this fashion. This does not occur from the oral ingestion of the drug.

This problem led a small biotech company near Albany, New York, to invent a method in which the AMP (d-amphetamine) cannot be activated unless it is in the human stomach or intestines. They achieved this by bonding a lysine compound to the d-AMP.

This bonding of an active drug to another compound alters its typical pattern of activation and is called a pro-drug by the FDA. In this form, the AMP is inactive and will remain so until it is swallowed. Then, a naturally occurring chemical in the stomach, intestine and blood supply splits the lysine from the d-AMP. And now the d-AMP can go to work and be absorbed into the blood stream.

The drug is designed in such a way that the d-AMP lasts 10–14 hours, typically. This delivery system greatly reduces the likely abuse potential of this version of AMP while providing for the desired longer time course of action from a single dose.

# Side Effects of Stimulants

The most common side effects people experience when taking a stimulant (MPH or AMP) are listed in order of greatest likelihood of occurrence:

- Insomnia, or trouble falling asleep.
- Loss of appetite, especially for the midday meal: some older children and teens perceive this as a benefit if they are trying to lose weight.
- Weight loss: again some older children and teens do not see this as an adverse effect, but as a positive effect if they are trying to lose weight.
- Headaches.
- Nausea, upset stomach, or stomachache.
- Anxiety: the research is somewhat mixed on whether stimulants worsen anxiety but enough studies have found this to be the case, particularly with children with ADHD, that it should continue to be listed as a possible adverse effect.
- Irritability, or being easily upset, angered, or prone to outbursts: just as often or more often, however, managing the ADHD can actually reduce problems with controlling one's emotion. As mentioned earlier, problems with regulating one's emotions are actually characteristic of ADHD, so treating the ADHD can often make this area of functioning better, not worse.
- Motor tics: stimulants may not cause these outright in patients unless they have a family history for tic disorders and thus are somewhat more vulnerable to develop a tic than are others without such a history. If tics are already present, they can be worsened in up to one-third of such cases, but in the remainder the tics remain unchanged or may even be improved.
- Increased muscle tension: though not very common, some people report sensations like they may have if they drink too much caffeine, such as tenseness of or frequent clenching of the jaw, muscle tension in the forehead, or generally feeling more taut in their posture.

The stimulants also increase heart rate and blood pressure slightly but generally no more so and often less than if you had just climbed a half-flight of stairs. You may have heard claims that these drugs increase the sensitivity to or risk for abusing other drugs, especially other stimulants. The vast majority of research does not support this claim. People who have taken ADHD medications like the stimulants for years, including children growing up with ADHD, were found to be no more likely to abuse drugs than were those not being treated. In fact in a few studies they were found to be less likely to do so, probably because the ADHD medication was controlling their impulsiveness.

You may have also heard that these drugs, especially the stimulants, might increase the likelihood of sudden death, usually from heart block (heart stops beating). In rare cases, strokes have occurred in people on these drugs. Although some people have died while taking a stimulant, these cases always involve other extenuating factors that alone can account for the sudden death. Those reasons include things such as a history of structural heart defects along with engaging in vigorous exercise just preceding the death. The available evidence actually shows that people on stimulants have a somewhat lower likelihood of sudden death than the general population (which is 1–7 people per every 100,000 people per year, depending on age).

This is probably because physicians routinely screen for heart problems before starting people on stimulants and, if discovered, usually do not use these medications. So those with the greatest likelihood of having heart problems if they took a stimulant are not prescribed them. Even so, physicians have been cautioned not to put people on stimulants if they have a history of sudden death in their family or a history of structural heart abnormalities, major arrhythmias, or other major cardiac problems. It also makes sense not to treat people with clinically or morbidly high blood pressure with a stimulant for the obvious reason that it can make the situation even more risky for them. The risk to otherwise healthy children and teens with ADHD is not significant, if there is any increased risk at all.

## Atomoxetine – A Nonstimulant

In 2003, the FDA approved the first nonstimulant drug for the management of child, teen, and adult ADHD, and the first new drug for ADHD in more than 25 years. That drug was atomoxetine, under the brand name Strattera®. It was the most studied ADHD drug before receiving FDA approval that has ever been brought to market. Randomized and double-blind studies were done involving more than 6,000 patients worldwide to thoroughly study the effectiveness, side effects, and safety of this medication. Now, as with the stimulants, millions of people worldwide take this medication for management of their ADHD.

As noted, AMP acts in the brain by increasing the amount of dopamine that is produced and expressed from the nerve cell when it is activated. To a lesser extent, it may also block the transport system by which the dopamine is normally reabsorbed back into that nerve cell after being released. MPH mainly acts by preventing this reabsorption of dopamine and so is known as a transport or reuptake blocker. Atomoxetine (ATX), in contrast, works by blocking the reabsorption of norepinephrine once it has been released. Like, MPH, it is a reuptake blocker, but it blocks the reuptake of a different neurochemical – norepinephrine. But some research shows that by doing this, ATX does result in an increase in dopamine outside nerve cells in certain parts of the brain, such as the frontal cortex.

ATX also differs from the stimulants, however, in that it does not affect the brain centers that are likely to be related to drug addiction or abuse. For this reason, the drug is called a nonstimulant. It is also why it is not classified as a controlled substance in the United States. Research shows that the drug has a low potential for abuse, meaning it is not preferred or liked by known drug addicts more than other psychiatric drugs such as antidepressants, which is to say addicts like it very little. The different means by which it acts in the brain can result in a different profile of potential side effects (adverse reactions) and possibly somewhat different benefits from this drug than what one sees with the stimulants.

ATX is nearly as effective for managing ADHD symptoms as are the stimulants, but not quite. The same percentage of patients appears to respond positively to both these classes of drugs (stimulants and nonstimulants), averaging about 75 percent of people responding. However, some studies suggest that while 50 percent of people respond positively to both types of medications, 25 percent may respond better to a stimulant than to ATX and the remaining

25 percent may respond better to ATX than to one of the stimulants. In other words, some people are unique responders who do better on one type of ADHD drug than on another. We should not be surprised at this result given that not all people are biologically identical especially in the organization and functioning of their brains. Some studies suggest that ATX may not produce quite as much improvement in ADHD symptoms as do the stimulants. But for some adults, the degree of improvement is sufficient to effectively manage their disorder while not necessarily producing the same types of side effects that one might get with a stimulant.

For instance, stimulants have been found in some studies to increase anxiety, nervous tics or nervous habits, and insomnia. Other studies have not found this to be the case, but the potential for such side effects remains. And in most forms, stimulants have the potential to be abused or diverted to others who were not prescribed the drug. ATX does not adversely affect anxiety, may even reduce it significantly, does not worsen tics or nervous habits, and does not typically result in insomnia.

The issue that physicians face in daily practice with ADHD patients is therefore not which drug works better, but which drug is best suited to which individual patient given that patient's unique profile of characteristics. Having many different drugs, just like having many different delivery systems, lets physicians better tailor their treatment to the uniqueness of each patient. With ATX, your student can expect it to take longer to adjust and find the right dose than is the case with a stimulant, primarily because it takes longer for the body to adjust to the side effects of drugs like ATX. For this reason, physicians may leave patients on a particular dose a bit longer than with a stimulant before adjusting the dose upward.

## ATX Side Effects

The most common side effects for ATX are:

- Nausea or vomiting
- Dry mouth
- Dizziness or light-headedness
- Constipation
- Sweating
- Decreased libido (sex drive) or erectile dysfunction
- Sweating
- Insomnia (far less common than with the stimulants)
- Irritability (same as with the stimulants – some patients actually report improvement in their mood or emotional self-control while on this medication)

Although ATX can also increase heart rate and blood pressure, it does so less than the stimulants. It does carry an exceptionally rare chance of liver complications that occurred once in every million people treated (4 cases out of 4.5 million treated to date). This reaction seems to result from a rare autoimmune reaction to the drug in which the body's immune system attacks and inflames the outer layers of the liver. More recently, two of these cases were discounted as being due to other factors not related to the drug. So the risk for this side effect is now about 1 in every 2–3 million people treated. But to be safe, people with a history of liver damage or other liver problems may want to avoid using ATX.

The package insert for ATX contains a warning of a possibility of increased suicidal thinking from this drug, but not suicide attempts, and only in children. This side effect is highly questionable given the lack of rigor with which the information on which it is based was collected in the initial clinical trials for this drug. This problem of increased suicidal thinking was not found for teens and adults with ADHD taking ATX. Also, recent research has found that people with ADHD who are off medication have a far higher rate of suicidal thinking and attempts than do those who are taking either ATX or a stimulant medication. These findings suggest that taking these medicines for ADHD may actually reduce the risk for suicidal thinking and attempts.

## Antihypertensive Drugs

Two other medicines are sometimes used to treat ADHD, but they should be considered "last choice" medicines to be used only if other ADHD medicines are not proving satisfactory. Both originated as drugs used to treat high blood pressure, called antihypertensive drugs. One is clonidine, which works as alpha-adrenergic enhancer. Some nerve cells in the brain have little portholes on them called alpha-2 receptors. These drugs seem to act to reduce or close off these portholes, resulting in stronger or more effective nerve signals in those cells. At low doses, this drug appears to stimulate inhibitory systems in the brain.

The FDA approved an extended-release version of clonidine, clonidine ER (Kapvay®), in 2010 as a treatment for ADHD in children ages 6–17 years. However, physicians can use it "off-label" outside of this age range, such as for adults with ADHD. It can be used alone or combined with stimulants. The drug is not as effective as other ADHD medicines, so it is sometimes used to treat ADHD when it coexists with another disorder such as conduct or antisocial problems or irritability and anger. It can also treat tic disorders, sleep disturbances, and may reduce anxiety.

Regular clonidine is fast acting. But the extended-release version approved for ADHD can last much longer.

The most common side effect of clonidine is sedation, which tends to subside with continued treatment. It can also result in reduce blood pressure, called hypotension, and sometimes results in complaints of dry mouth, vivid dreams, depression, and confusion. Unlike other ADHD medicines, this one cannot be stopped abruptly. It requires slow tapering over several days to weeks. The drug should not be used if your student is taking beta-blockers or calcium channel blockers. Experts recommend blood pressure monitoring for anyone using these drugs for treating ADHD, when starting or when tapering off clonidine, and when doses are being increased.

Another antihypertensive drug used for ADHD management is guanfacine. In 2009, the FDA approved an extended-release version, guanfacine ER (Intuniv®) for the treatment of ADHD in people who are 6–17 years. Again, physicians can use it off-label with adults if they think it essential to do so. The drug can be given alone or in combination with either of the stimulant medicines discussed earlier.

Some advantages of guanfacine over clonidine include less sedation, a longer duration of action and less risk of cardiovascular problems. This drug can result in minor decreases in blood pressure and pulse rate. Other side effects include sedation, irritability, and depression. Again this medication probably is not as effective as stimulants or ATX. Its benefit may be in helping to treat coexisting disorders with ADHD, such as anger and aggression, and in reducing highly impulsive or hyperactive behavior.

You and your student should be aware that far less research has been conducted on the use of these two antihypertensive drugs to treat ADHD than with the stimulants or ATX. They were FDA approved mainly for children based on the limited research available. Because of the limited amount of research, these drugs are considered last choice options for managing ADHD. The other ADHD medicines above should be tried first.

# References and
# Evidence Base

Barkley, R. A. (Ed.) (2015). *Attention Deficit Hyperactivity Disorder: A Handbook for Diagnosis and Treatment (4th Edition)*. New York: Guilford Press.

Barkley, R. A., Shelton, T. L., Crosswait, C., Moorehouse, M., Fletcher, K., Barrett, S., et al. (2000). Multi-method psycho-educational intervention for preschool children with disruptive behavior: Preliminary results at post-treatment. *Journal of Abnormal Child Psychiatry and Psychology, 41*, 319–332.

Bowman-Perrott, L., Davis, H., Vannest, K., Williams, L., Greenwood, C., & Parker, R. (2013). Academic benefits of peer tutoring: A meta-analytic review of single-case research. *School Psychology Review, 42*, 39–55.

Cooper, H., Robinson, J. C., & Patall, E. A. (2006). Does homework improve academic achievement? A synthesis of research, 1987–2003. *Review of Educational Research, 76*, 1–62.

DuPaul, G. J., Eckert, T. L., & Vilardo, B. (2012). The effects of school-based interventions for attention-deficit hyperactivity disorder: A meta-analysis 1996–2010. *School Psychology Review, 41*, 387–412.

DuPaul, G. J., Ervin, R. A., Hook, C. L., & McGoey, K. E. (1998). Peer tutoring for children with attention deficit hyperactivity disorder: Effects on classroom behavior and academic performance. *Journal of Applied Behavior Analysis, 31*, 579–592.

DuPaul, G. J., Jitendra, A. K., Volpe, R. J., Tresco, K. E., Lutz, G., Vile Junod, R. E., Cleary, K. S., Flammer, L. M., & Mannella, M. C. (2006). Consultation-based academic interventions for children with ADHD: Effects on reading and mathematics achievement. *Journal of Abnormal Child Psychology, 34*, 633–646.

DuPaul, G. J., & Stoner, G. (2014). *ADHD in the Schools (3rd ed.)*. New York: Guilford Press.

DuPaul, G. J., & Weyandt, L. L. (2006). School-based interventions for children and adolescents with attention-deficit/hyperactivity disorder: Enhancing academic and behavioral outcomes. *Education & Treatment of Children, 29*, 341–358.

Evans, J. H., Ferre, L., Ford, L. A., & Green, J. L. (1995). Decreasing attention deficit hyperactivity disorder symptoms utilizing an automated classroom reinforcement device. *Psychology in the Schools, 32*, 210–219.

Evans, S. W., Pelham, W., & Grudberg, M. V. (1994). The efficacy of notetaking to improve behavior and comprehension of adolescents with attention deficit hyperactivity disorder. *Exceptionality, 5(1)*, 1–17.

Fabiano, G. A., Pelham, W. E., Gnagy, E. M., Burrows-MacLean, L., Coles, E., Chacko, A., Wymbs, B. T., Walker, K. S., Arnold, F., Garefino, A., Keenan, J. K., Onyango, A. N., Hoffman, M. T., Massetti, G. M., & Robb, J. A., (2007). The single and combined effects of multiple intensities of behavior modification and methylphenidate for children with attention deficit hyperactivity disorder in a classroom setting. *School Psychology Review, 36*, 195–216.

Fabiano, G. A., Pelham, W. E., Karmazin, K., Kreher, J., Panahon, C. J., & Carlson, C. (2008). A group contingency program to improve the behavior of elementary school students in a cafeteria. *Behavior Modification, 32*, 121–132.

Fabiano, G. A., Vujnovic, R. K., Pelham, W. E., Waschbusch, D. A., Massetti, G.M., Pariseau, M. E., Naylor, J., Yu, J., Robins, M., Cronefix, T., Greiner, A. R., & Volker, M. (2010). Enhancing the effectiveness of special education programming for children with attention deficit hyperactivity disorder using a daily report card. *School Psychology Review, 39*, 219–239.

Gast, D. C., & Nelson, C. M. (1977). Time-out in the classroom: Implications for special education. *Exceptional Children, 43*, 461–464.

Gordon, M., Thomason, D., Cooper, S., & Ivers, C. L. (1990). Nonmedical treatment of ADHD/hyperactivity: The attention training system. *Journal of School Psychology, 29*, 151–159.

Hoff, K. E., & DuPaul, G. J. (1998). Reducing disruptive behavior in general education classrooms: The use of self-management strategies. *School Psychology Review, 27*, 290–303.

Hoza, B. & Smith, A. L. (2015). Is aerobic physical activity a viable management strategy for ADHD? *The ADHD Report, 23(2)*, 1–5.

Jurbergs, N., Palcic, J. L., & Kelley, M. L. (2008). School-home notes with and without response cost: Increasing attention and academic performance in low-income children with attention-deficit/hyperactivity disorder. *School Psychology Quarterly, 22*, 358–379.

Jurbergs, N., Palcic, J. L., & Kelley, M. L. (2010). Daily behavior report cards with and without home-based consequences: Improving classroom behavior in low income, African American children with ADHD. *Child and Family Behavior Therapy, 32*, 177–195.

Kelley, M. L. (1990). *School–Home Notes: Promoting Children's Classroom Success.* New York: Guilford Press.

Mautone, J. A., DuPaul, G. J., & Jitendra, A. K. (2005). The effects of computer-assisted instruction on the mathematics performance and classroom behavior of children with ADHD. *Journal of Attention Disorders, 9*, 301–312.

McGoey, K. E., & DuPaul, G. J. (2000). Token reinforcement and response cost procedures: Reducing the disruptive behavior of preschool children with ADHD. *School Psychology Quarterly, 15*, 330–343.

Meyer, K. (2007). Improving homework in adolescents with attention-deficit/hyperactivity disorder: Self vs. parent monitoring of homework behavior and study skills. *Child and Family Behavior Therapy, 29*, 25–42.

Nelson, J. R., Benner, G. J., & Mooney, P. (2008). *Instructional Practices for Students with Behavioral Disorders: Strategies for Reading, Writing, and Math.* New York: Guilford Press.

Ota, K. R., & DuPaul, G. J. (2002). Task engagement and mathematics performance in children with attention deficit hyperactivity disorder: Effects of supplemental computer intervention. *School Psychology Quarterly, 17(3)*, 242–257.

Owens, J. S., Holdaway, A. S., Zoromski, A. K., Evans, S. W., Himawan, L. K., Girio-Herrera, E., & Murphy, C. E. (2012). Incremental benefits of a daily report card intervention over time for youth with disruptive behavior. *Behavior Therapy, 43*, 848–861.

Pagani, L., Tremblay, R., Vitaro, F., Boulerice, B., & McDuff, P. (2001). Effects of grade retention on academic performance and behavioral development. *Development and Psychopathology, 13*, 297–315.

Pfiffner, L. J. (2011). *All about ADHD: The Complete Practical Guide for Classroom Teachers (2nd Edition).* New York: Scholastic.

Pfiffner, L., & DuPaul, G. J. (2015). Treatment of ADHD in school settings. In R. A. Barkley (Ed.), *Attention Deficit Hyperactivity Disorder: A Handbook for Diagnosis and Treatment (4th edition).* New York: Guilford Press.

Pontifex, M. B., Saliba, B. J., Raine, L. B., Picchietti, D. L., & Hillman, C. H. (2013). Exercise improves behavioral, neurocognitive, and scholastic performance in children with attention-deficit/hyperactivity disorder. *Journal of Pediatrics, 162*, 543–551.

Power, T. J., Karustis, J. L., & Habboushe, D. F. (2001). *Homework Success for Children with ADHD: A Family–School Intervention Program.* New York: Guilford Press.

Reid, R., Trout, A. L., & Schartz, M. (2005). Self-regulation interventions for children with attention deficit/hyperactivity disorder. *Exceptional Children, 71*, 361–377.

Sheridan, S. M., Welch, M., & Ormi, S. F. (1996). Is consultation effective? A review of outcome research. *Remedial and Special Education, 17*, 341–354.

Spencer, V. G. (2006). Peer tutoring and students with emotional or behavioral disorders: A review of the literature. *Behavioral Disorders, 31*, 204–222.

# Web Resources

www.Ldonline.org

www.Chadd.org

www.Help4adhd.org

www.Caddra.ca

http://www.teachadhd.ca/teaching-children-with-adhd/Pages/default.aspx

A fine website chock full of ideas on curriculum development for ADHD students and behavior management strategies.

What is Teach ADHD.ca?

"The TeachADHD project began at <u>Brain and Behaviour Research</u> program at <u>The Hospital for Sick Children</u> and has evolved through the hospital's Community Health Systems Resource Group's "Teach for Success" initiative. The project's mission is to make available to teachers relevant educational material stemming from current ADHD research in order to improve the learning outcomes of all students. It is the intention of TeachADHD to present only information that is supported by substantiated research. All materials developed for this project have been evaluated by teachers for its educational relevance." Information was developed using multiple organizations including school systems around Toronto, the Hospital for Sick Children Brain and Behavior section, TVOntario, and others."

The following subpage is a fine review of medications, from the Canadian perspective:

http://www.teachadhd.ca/teaching-children-with-adhd/Pages/Home-and-School-Connection.aspx

**British Columbia Department of Education**

http://www.bced.gov.bc.ca/specialed/adhd/

**Resources from Sandra Reif**

https://www.pinterest.com/sandrarief/add-adhd-for-teachers/

**Successful Schools**

http://successfulschools.org/wp-content/uploads/trip_guide_adhd_interventions.pdf?phpMyAdmin=168c4a6ce7f3t76b9b6da

**National Association of School Psychologists**
http://www.nasponline.org/resources/handouts/05-1_S8-05_ADHD_Classroom_
Interventions.pdf and http://www.nasponline.org/resources/handouts/special%20needs%20
template.pdf

**Child Development Institute, LLC**
http://childdevelopmentinfo.com/learning/learning_disabilities/teacher/

**National Association of Special Education Teachers – Classroom Management of ADHD**
http://images.pcmac.org/Uploads/MuscleShoals/MuscleShoals/Divisions/
DocumentsCategories/Documents/Classroom_Mngt_Techniques_ADHD.pdf

**Resources at HelpGuide**
http://www.helpguide.org/articles/add-adhd/teaching-students-with-adhd-attention-deficit-
disorder.htm

**US Dept. of Education**
http://www2.ed.gov/rschstat/research/pubs/adhd/adhd-teaching_pg4.html
and http://www2.ed.gov/rschstat/research/pubs/adhd/adhd-teaching-2008.pdf

**Intervention Central**
http://www.interventioncentral.org/behavioral-interventions/challenging-students/school-
wide-strategies-managing-hyperactivity

**Additude Magazine**
http://www.additudemag.com/adhd/article/6006.html

**New Ideas**
http://newideas.net/pdf/101-classroom-interventions-elementary.pdf

**About ADHD**
http://add.about.com/od/childrenandteens/a/adhd-classroom.htm

**Education World**
http://www.educationworld.com/a_issues/issues148c.shtml

**Teaching Channel**
https://www.teachingchannel.org/videos/teaching-adhd-students
Provides videos for helping teachers with classroom management problems with ADHD
students.

**Ideas for Teaching Children with ADHD – Leah Davies, M.Ed.**
http://www.kellybear.com/TeacherArticles/TeacherTip49.html31

---

For your convenience, you may download a PDF version of the handouts
in this book from our dedicated website: go.pesi.com/barkley

# Other Books By
# Russell Barkley

***Executive Functions:*** *What They Are, How They Work, and Why They Evolved*
Russell A. Barkley

***Barkley Deficits in Executive Functioning Scale (BDEFS)***
Russell A. Barkley

***Barkley Deficits in Executive Functioning Scale - Children and Adolescents (BDEFS-CA)***
Russell A. Barkley

***Barkley Adult ADHD Rating Scale-IV (BAARS-IV)***
Russell A. Barkley

***Barkley Functional Impairment Scale (BFIS)***
Russell A. Barkley

***Barkley Functional Impairment Scale - Children and Adolescents (BFIS-CA)***
Russell A. Barkley

***Taking Charge of Adult ADHD***
Russell A. Barkley with Christine M. Benton

***ADHD and the Nature of Self-Control***
Russell A. Barkley

***ADHD in Adults:*** *What the Science Says*
Russell A. Barkley, Kevin R. Murphy, and Mariellen Fischer

***Attention-Deficit Hyperactivity Disorder:***
*A Handbook for Diagnosis and Treatment, Third Edition*
Russell A. Barkley

***Defiant Children:*** *A Clinician's Manual for Assessment and Parent Training, Third Edition*
Russell A. Barkley

***Defiant Teens:*** *A Clinician's Manual for Assessment and Family Intervention*
Russell A. Barkley, Gwenyth H. Edwards, and Arthur L. Robin

***Taking Charge of ADHD, Revised Edition:*** *The Complete, Authoritative Guide for Parents*
Russell A. Barkley

***Your Defiant Child:*** *Eight Steps to Better Behavior, 2nd Edition*
Russell A. Barkley

***Your Defiant Teen:*** *10 Steps to Resolve Conflict and Rebuild Your Relationship*
Russell A. Barkley and Arthur L. Robin with Christine M. Benton

Made in the USA
Las Vegas, NV
10 October 2024

96629343R00059